Chemistry
100 LABORATORY MANUAL

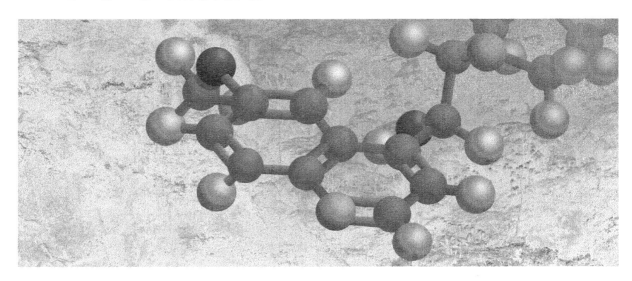

Introduction to Chemistry • LABORATORY MANUAL and LECTURE SUPPLEMENTS

SECOND EDITION

Michael Hailu • Ludwig Sprandel

Biological and Physical Sciences Department
Columbus State Community College

Custom Publishing

Boston Burr Ridge, IL Dubuque, IA Madison, WI New York San Francisco St. Louis
Bangkok Bogotá Caracas Lisbon London Madrid
Mexico City Milan New Delhi Seoul Singapore Sydney Taipei Toronto

Chemistry 100
Introduction to Chemistry
LABORATORY MANUAL and LECTURE SUPPLEMENTS

McGraw-Hill's Custom Publishing consists of products that are produced from camera-ready copy. Peer review, class testing, and accuracy are primarily the responsibility of the author(s).

90 TPS TPS 098765

ISBN 0-07-287955-6

Editor: Nicole Young
Production Editor: Lynn Nagel
Cover Design: Fairfax Hutter
Printer/Binder: Total Printing Systems

ACKNOWLEDGMENTS

The following chemistry faculty members of the Biological and Physical Sciences Department of Columbus State Community College contributed material to this manual.

William Griffiths

Marc Lord

Michael Rennekamp

TABLE OF CONTENTS

LABORATORY MANUAL — EXPERIMENTS

LECTURE SUPPLEMENT — COURSE OBJECTIVES

LECTURE SUPPLEMENT - REVIEW SHEETS

LECTURE SUPPLEMENT - WORKSHEETS

LABORATORY MANUAL

EXPERIMENTS

INTRODUCTION TO THE LABORATORY

Objective

Your objective in this laboratory is to learn important safety rules and basic techniques that are necessary for working safely and efficiently in a chemistry lab. You will inventory the equipment in your assigned locker, view a safety video, and practice some lab procedures.

Introduction

An academic chemistry laboratory is the place where students perform experiments for educational purposes. These experiments illustrate and enhance theoretical and descriptive material being studied in chemistry lecture. It is essential that students perform their experiments in a safe manner, and it is important that they work efficiently in the laboratory.

To ensure safety in the laboratory, students must follow certain safety rules and procedures. These will be reviewed in the video *Starting with Safety*. While there are many aspects to lab safety, safety equipment and waste disposal are of prime importance. Students must wear their own splash-resistant safety goggles when working in the lab. Students must know the locations of the shower, eyewash, fire extinguisher, and fire blanket and how to operate them. Waste and excess chemicals must be disposed of in proper waste containers, and never in the sink or trash can. As part of their safety training, students will be required to complete a safety quiz and sign a safety agreement.

To work efficiently in the lab, students must be familiar with the identity and use of various pieces of equipment and glassware found in the laboratory. To accomplish this, students will inventory the equipment in their assigned locker and practice some lab procedures such as using a balance, reading a graduated cylinder, and lighting a Bunsen burner.

In order to have a safe, productive, and enjoyable lab experience, students should read the experiments ahead of time, work at a comfortable pace, and use common sense at all times in the laboratory. Finally, students must remember to apply what they learn in this lab to all of the experiments that they perform. Safety and the use of proper lab techniques are ongoing concerns in this course.

Procedure

A. Equipment inventory

1. An equipment locker will be assigned to you. Remove the contents of the locker, placing all the items on the lab bench.

2. Using the **CHEMISTRY LOCKER INVENTORY** sheet and the **LABORATORY EQUIPMENT** sheet, make an inventory of your equipment. Note the correct name of each piece of equipment, and return each item to your locker as you check it off the list.

3. Replace any broken or missing items with equipment from the lab supply cabinet. Return extra items and any equipment not on the inventory list to the place indicated by your instructor.

4. Note that students in other courses will also use your locker. Therefore, it is important that you clean your glassware before leaving the lab.

B. Laboratory safety

1. Your instructor will show a video entitled *Starting with Safety*, which reviews the safety rules that are important for your laboratory.

2. While watching the video, complete the **Safety Quiz**. Note that the quiz is correlated to the various sections of the video. When requested, submit the quiz to your instructor.

3. Your instructor will then discuss lab safety and show you the location of the shower, eyewash, fire extinguisher, and fire blanket.

4. Using the **CHEMISTRY LABORATORY SAFETY RULES/AGREEMENT** sheet, carefully read the summarized **Safety Rules** that are pertinent to the laboratory and complete and sign both copies of the **Safety Agreement**. When requested, submit one of the copies to your instructor.

C. Laboratory techniques

1. Your instructor will demonstrate a number of lab
   procedures that you will be required to perform as this
   course progresses.

   a. Using a balance; determining mass by difference
   b. Using a graduated cylinder; reading the meniscus
   c. Lighting and adjusting a Bunsen burner
   d. Heating a test tube with a Bunsen burner
   e. Heating a crucible or beaker; using the ring stand and
      iron ring
   f. Disposing of waste and excess chemicals

2. Practice using the balance, graduated cylinder, and Bunsen
   burner.

CHEMISTRY LOCKER INVENTORY

1 – apron or lab coat

1 – beaker, 100-mL

1 – beaker, 250-mL

1 – beaker, 400-mL

1 – beaker, 600-mL

1 – Bunsen burner with tubing

1 – clamp

1 – clay triangle

1 – crucible with cover

1 – Erlenmeyer flask, 50-mL

1 – Erlenmeyer flask, 125-mL

1 – Erlenmeyer flask, 250-mL

1 – funnel

1 – graduated cylinder, 10-mL

1 – graduated cylinder, 50-mL

1 – graduated cylinder, 100-mL

1 – iron ring

2 – medicine droppers

1 – mortar and pestle

4 – rubber stoppers, size 0

1 – scoop

1 – stirring rod

1 – test tube holder

1 – test tube rack

9 – test tubes, 16x150-mm

3 – test tubes, 25x200-mm

1 – tongs

1 – towel

1 – watch glass

1 – water bottle

1 – wax pencil

1 – wire screen

LABORATORY EQUIPMENT

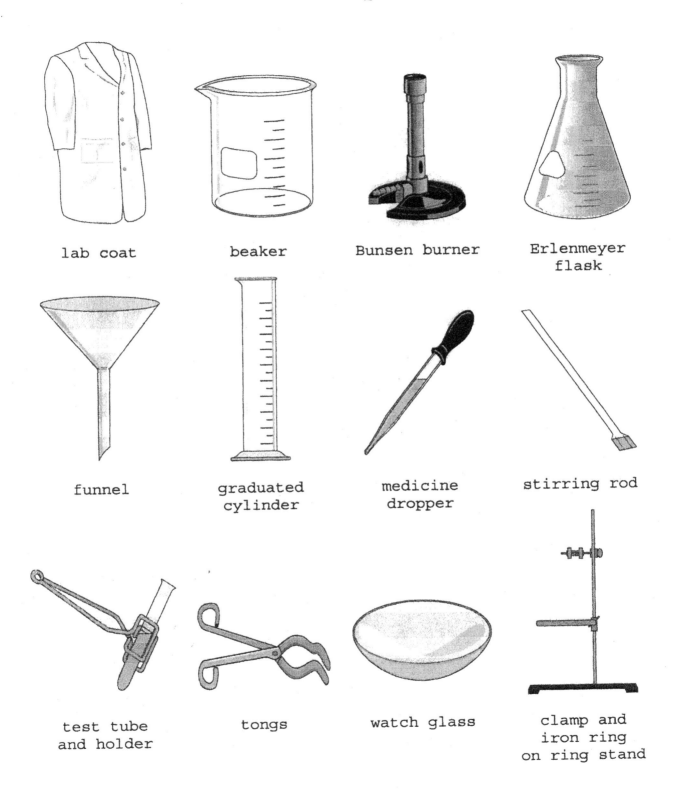

lab coat

beaker

Bunsen burner

Erlenmeyer flask

funnel

graduated cylinder

medicine dropper

stirring rod

test tube and holder

tongs

watch glass

clamp and iron ring on ring stand

CHEMISTRY LABORATORY SAFETY AGREEMENT

In order to decrease the potential for injury in the laboratory, you the student will review the following points and sign a form that states that you have read and understand them and agree to comply with them. Failure to comply with any of these points may mean that you will be dismissed from the lab immediately and will not be allowed to make it up. Students will not be allowed to participate in the lab until the agreement is signed. The form needs to be signed and dated and given to the instructor. Refer to these guidelines as often as necessary.

We of Columbus State Community College will keep your signed agreement until the end of the quarter. In the even of an accident or other incident, we will keep your signed agreement for a period of 30 years.

SAFETY RULES

1. Absolutely no unauthorized experiments should be attempted.
2. Safety glasses must be worn at all times in the laboratory.
3. Know the location of safety equipment and how to operate it.
4. Wear sensible clothing. Aprons must be worn at all times.
5. While in the laboratory, never put anything in your mouth.
6. Use the fume hood when necessary.
7. Keep the laboratory clean.
8. Use only equipment that is in good condition.
9. Never work alone.
10. Dispose of waste and excess materials in the proper manner.
11. Avoid touching hot objects.
12. Use extreme caution when inserting glass into stoppers.
13. Handle chemicals with caution.
    a. Read the labels carefully.
    b. Use only when is needed.
    c. Leave chemicals in their proper place.
    d. All spills must be cleaned up immediately.
14. Report immediately all accidents that cause injury, no matter how minor, to the laboratory instructor.
15. No visitors allowed in the laboratory.
16. When in the laboratory, **THINK** and use common sense and good judgment about what you are doing at all times!

METRIC MEASUREMENTS

Objective

The objective of this experiment is to measure lengths, masses, and volumes using metric units. In the laboratory, you will become proficient with the use of the meter stick, the electronic balance, and the graduated cylinder.

Introduction

Measurement is the comparison of a physical quantity to be measured with a unit of measurement. A measurement determines the quantity, dimensions, or extent of something in comparison to a specific unit. A unit is a definite quantity adopted as a reference standard. The result of a measurement consists of two parts – a numerical value followed by a specific unit.

The metric system is a system of measurement that was established in France in the 1790s. It consists of a set of base units that correspond to various physical quantities to be measured and a group of prefixes that are used with each base unit to form a series of units having different sizes. Each prefix corresponds to a power of 10. Therefore, each metric unit is related in size to other units of the same type by a power of 10, making the metric system a decimal system of measurement. Use of the metric system gradually spread from France to many other countries and also to the scientific community. The modern version of the metric system is called the International System of Units, or SI. It is the official system of measurement used by most countries in the world and the system of choice of scientists.

The base metric units that will be studied in this lab are the meter (m), the gram (g), and the liter (L), which are used for measuring length, mass, and volume, respectively. The metric prefixes centi- (c), signifying 0.01 or 10^{-2}, and milli- (m), signifying 0.001 or 10^{-3}, will be used with these base units to form units such as the centimeter (cm) and the milliliter (mL). To establish a working knowledge of these metric units, you will perform a number of basis laboratory measurements using the meter stick, the electronic balance, and the graduated cylinder.

Every measurement has a degree of uncertainty associated with it that the person making the measurement should strive to reduce to an acceptable level. An experiment is often repeated several times to obtain a replicate set of measurements for comparison. The reproducibility of results obtained by the same experimental method is termed precision. Using a set of individual measurements, an average of the measurements, called the mean, is calculated. The mean is obtained by adding the individual measurements and dividing the result by the number of measurements. For a series of 3 measurements x_1, x_2, and x_3, the mean, x_{av}, is given by the following expression.

$$x_{av} = (x_1 + x_2 + x_3)/3$$

The difference between any individual measurement and the mean is used to express the precision of the measurement. The deviation of a measurement x_i from the mean is the absolute value of the difference between x_i and the mean.

$$\text{deviation for } x_i = |x_i - x_{av}|$$

The relative deviation is obtained by multiplying the quotient of the deviation for a measured quantity and the mean by 100%.

$$\text{relative deviation for } x_i = (|x_i - x_{av}|/x_{av}) \times 100\%$$

The relative deviation is one method of expressing the precision of a measured quantity.

The closeness of a single measurement to the true value, x_{true}, is called accuracy. The difference between a measurement x_i and x_{true} is the error of the measurement.

$$\text{error in } x_i = x_i - x_{true}$$

Note that accuracy, which compares a measured quantity to the true value, is not the same as precision, which compares one measured quantity with the others. The true value is seldom known; the reason why we do experiments is to determine a value for a quantity. Thus, it is difficult to arrive at an estimate of the error of a measurement. The relative error is obtained by multiplying the quotient of the error in a measured quantity and the true value by 100%.

$$\text{relative error in } x_i = ((x_i - x_{true})/x_{true}) \times 100\%$$

The relative error is one method of expressing the accuracy of a measured quantity.

Errors in measured quantities fall into two broad categories - determinate errors and indeterminate errors. Determinate errors are systematic errors whose sources are assignable, such as an instrumental error or an error in the experimental method. Determinate errors affect the accuracy of the measurement. A determinate error will usually affect a given physical measurement in one particular direction.

Indeterminate errors are random errors, which means that they cannot be easily identified. These types of errors usually do not affect a given measurement in the same direction all the time. One common source of indeterminate error is the variation in the experimental technique of the investigator. Given a sufficient number of measurements of the same quantity, this type of error tends to average out, and the average value may approach the true value. The magnitude of this type of error is reflected in the precision of the measurement.

Materials

table salt (sodium chloride, NaCl) (6 g per group)

meter sticks (1 per group)
unknown samples for mass determination (1 per group)

Precautions

Use normal laboratory safety precautions. Since the table salt is used only for observational purposes, it does not need to be disposed of in a waste container. Return it to the original sample container.

Procedure

It is recommended that students work in groups of 2 or 3 for this experiment.

A. Measuring length

1. Observe the markings on a meter stick. The meter stick is divided into 100 numbered increments. What is the length of one of these numbered increments, which is 1/100 or 0.01 of a meter? If you observe closely, you will notice that each of the 100 numbered increments is divided into 10 un-numbered increments. Therefore, there are 1000 of these un-numbered increments on the meter stick. What is the length of one of these un-numbered increments, which is 1/1000 or 0.001 of a meter?

2. Use the meter stick to answer the following questions.

   a. Find the mark on the meter stick that represents 65 centimeters. How many millimeters are there in 65 centimeters? How many meters?

   b. Find the mark on the meter stick that represents 0.95 meter. How many centimeters are there in 0.95 meters? How many millimeters?

   c. How many meters are there in 170 centimeters? How many millimeters?

3. Measure the length, the width, and the height of your laboratory table in centimeters. What is the area of the tabletop in square centimeters? What is the volume of the lab table in cubic centimeters?

B. Measuring mass

1. Obtain an object of unknown mass from the dispensing table and determine its mass to the nearest 0.01 gram. Record the mass and the code number of the unknown. Return the unknown to the dispensing table.

2. Measure out a sample of water using the following steps.

   a. Determine the mass of a 250-mL beaker to the nearest 0.01 gram. This mass is called the tare.

   b. Carefully measure 25.0 milliliters of water in a graduated cylinder. Transfer the water to the 250-mL beaker.

   c. Determine the gross mass of the beaker and the water. Calculate the net mass of the water.

3. Measure out 5.23 grams of table salt on a piece of weighing paper. Record the gross, tare, and net masses. Retain the measured sample for inspection by your instructor. The sample may be returned to the original container after inspection.

C. Measuring volume

1. Measure out 6 milliliters of water in both the 10-mL and the 100-mL graduated cylinders. Remember that volumes are measured at the bottom of the meniscus. Record each volume to the proper number of significant figures. Note which cylinder gives the more precise measurement.

2. Measure out 60 milliliters of water in a 250-mL beaker. Pour the water into a 100-mL graduated cylinder and read the volume to the proper number of significant figures. Note which measuring device - the beaker or the graduated cylinder - gives the more accurate measurement.

1 $\times 10^{2}$ $\times 10^{-3}$

m. cm mm

DENSITY

Objective

Your objective in this lab is to determine densities for various samples of matter. You will use different techniques to measure volume, and you will investigate a graphical procedure for calculating density.

Introduction

Density is a physical property of matter defined as mass per unit volume. In mathematical terms, the density of a sample of matter is related to its mass and volume by the equation

$$\text{density} = \text{mass/volume} \quad \text{or} \quad d = m/v \, .$$

Common metric units for density are g/mL and g/cm^3. Since a density value is the mass of a unit volume of a substance, it gives an indication of the compactness of that substance.

The density of a sample of matter is a characteristic property of the chemical substance that makes up the sample. It does not depend on the size or the shape of the sample. The densities of liquids and solids vary slightly with temperature, while the densities of gases depend strongly on both temperature and pressure. Since each chemical substance has a characteristic density value, densities can be useful in trying to identify substances.

To determine experimentally the density of a sample of matter, the mass and the volume of the sample must be measured. Density is then calculated using the above equation. In a modern chemistry lab, mass is usually measured using an electronic balance. You will use a balance that is capable of determining mass to a precision of 0.01 g. The mass of an inert solid can be obtained by placing it directly on the balance pan. For a liquid or a gas, however, a container must be used. The mass of the liquid or gaseous sample is then obtained as the difference between the mass of the container and sample and the mass of the empty container.

The technique used to measure volume will depend on factors such as the physical state and the geometric shape of the sample. For a solid sample that has a regular geometric shape, the volume can be obtained by calculation using the measured dimensions of the sample. The volume of a cylindrical sample, for example, can be calculated using the equation

$$V = \pi r^2 h \ ,$$

where π = 3.1416, r is the radius of the cylinder, and h is its height. When a solid is submerged in a liquid, it will displace a volume of the liquid equal to its volume. This displacement technique provides a reliable means for measuring the volume of a solid sample that has an irregular geometric shape. For this technique to work, the solid must be insoluble in the liquid, and it must be completely submerged. Finally, the volume of a liquid sample can be determined directly using a graduated cylinder.

Materials

assorted cylindrical metal samples (1 per student)
assorted rubber stoppers (1 per student)
unknown liquid sample (25-30 mL per student)

small metric rulers with mm and cm markings (1 per student)
CRC Handbook of Chemistry and Physics (1 per 4 or 5 students)

Precautions

Use standard laboratory safety precautions. All volume and dimension measurements must be made very carefully in order to ensure accuracy in the density calculations.

Procedure

It is recommended that students work individually for this experiment.

A. Density of a solid sample with a regular shape
   (metal cylinder)

   1. Obtain a cylindrical metal sample from your instructor. Record the chemical identity and give a brief description (shape, color, etc.) of the sample.

   2. Determine the mass of the sample to the nearest 0.01 g. It may be placed directly on the balance pan.

3. Using a metric ruler, carefully measure to the nearest 0.01 cm the height and the diameter of the metal cylinder. Calculate the radius of the cylinder by dividing the diameter by 2.

4. Calculate the volume of the metal cylinder in cm^3.

5. Calculate the density of the metal sample in g/cm^3.

6. Return the metal cylinder to your instructor.

B. Density of a solid sample with an irregular shape (rubber stopper)

1. Obtain a rubber stopper from your instructor. Give a brief description (shape, color, etc.) of the sample.

2. Determine the mass of the sample to the nearest 0.01 g. It may be placed directly on the balance pan.

3. Fill a 100-mL graduated cylinder approximately halfway with water. Record the volume of the water to the nearest 0.1 mL.

4. Carefully slide the stopper into the graduated cylinder. Try to avoid splashing the water. Make sure that the stopper is completely submerged in the water and that no bubbles adhere to it. Record the volume for the water and the stopper to the nearest 0.1 mL.

5. Determine the volume of the stopper in mL by calculating the volume of water that it displaces.

6. Calculate the density of the rubber stopper in g/mL.

7. Return the stopper to your instructor.

C. Density of a liquid sample

1. Determine the mass of a dry 50-mL graduated cylinder to the nearest 0.01 g.

2. Obtain 25 to 30 mL of the unknown liquid sample in the graduated cylinder. Measure the mass of the cylinder and liquid sample to the nearest 0.01 g.

3. Calculate the mass of the liquid sample.

4. Measure the liquid volume to the nearest 0.1 mL.

5. Calculate the density of the liquid sample in g/mL.

6. Dispose of the liquid sample in the proper waste container.

D. Graphical determination of density - a collaborative exercise

1. Record the mass and the volume of the rubber stopper that you used in part B.

2. Consult with other students and obtain masses and volumes for 3 additional rubber stoppers that are different in size from the one that you used.

3. Plot the 4 mass-volume data points. Draw a straight line passing through the 0-0 point that best represents these data points.

4. Mark 2 points that are spaced widely apart on this line. Do not use any of your data points or the 0-0 point for this purpose.

5. Record the mass and volume values corresponding to these points. Use these values to calculate the slope of your straight line as indicated on the data sheet.

COMPUTER LABORATORY

Objective

Your objective in this laboratory is to explore some topics in chemistry using computer technology. You will learn how to use three different tutorial programs, and you will review a number of chemistry lessons using these interactive programs.

Introduction

Learning chemistry can be a difficult and time-consuming challenge for many students. There are many excellent learning resources available for today's students to help them meet this challenge. One such resource is the computer. At the present time, computer technology is being extensively and effectively used for chemical education purposes.

Textbook publishers often provide supporting CDs with their chemistry books. These are correlated with the text, and they are designed to enhance the presentation of the subject matter. In addition to the CDs, publishers frequently have web sites that students gain access to when they purchase their texts. Again, the material on the web site supports and enhances the textbook.

The Internet is a valuable learning resource for chemistry students. The number of chemistry-related web sites available for students to use is staggering. With a small investment of time, a student can usually locate a substantial amount of information on any given topic in chemistry. Typically, the learning materials that students obtain via the Internet are of high quality, and they can effectively be used to supplement and enhance materials obtained in class.

Another application of computer technology in chemical education is the use of commercially-available chemistry tutorial programs. Typically, these programs are purchased by educational institutions and made available to large numbers of students through computer networks. These programs usually cover a wide range of chemistry topics, they are frequently quite interactive, and they often make extensive use of graphics and video to enhance the presentation of the material.

In this computer laboratory, you will work with three of these chemistry tutorial programs – *Comprehensive Chemistry*, *Concentrated Chemical Concepts*, and *Exploring Chemistry*. You will learn how to use the programs, and you will be given the opportunity to review a number of their lessons. Lists of the general chemistry lessons contained in these programs are included at the end of this laboratory write-up.

Procedure

1. Review the lists of the general chemistry lessons that are available in the *Comprehensive Chemistry*, the *Concentrated Chemical Concepts*, and the *Exploring Chemistry* programs.

2. Go to the computer lab, **Nestor Hall room 232**, at the time indicated by your instructor.

3. Double-click on the **Chemistry** folder that is on the computer desktop. This will open a window that contains folders for various chemistry courses.

4. Double-click on the **Chem 100** folder. This will open a window that contains three icons labeled **Comprehensive Chemistry**, **Concentrated Concepts**, and **Explore Chemistry**.

5. Double-click on the icon of the program that you want to use. Select the **General Chemistry** topics. From the menu, select the lesson that you want to review.

6. Your instructor will explain how you should proceed in this lab. You may be allowed to work for the whole period on lessons that you select yourself. Your instructor may, however, assign some lessons that you will be required to complete.

7. At the end of the laboratory, please be sure to exit the chemistry program you are using and return to the computer desktop.

COMPUTER LABORATORY

Name _____

Date _____

Prelaboratory Assignment

1. Using the list of topics for *Comprehensive Chemistry*, select three lessons you would like to review in this lab.

2. Using the list of topics for *Concentrated Chemical Concepts*, select three lessons you would like to review in this lab.

3. Using the list of topics for *Exploring Chemistry*, select three lessons you would like to review in this lab.

COMPUTER LABORATORY

Name _____

Date _____

Laboratory Report

Results

A. *Comprehensive Chemistry*

    1. List the lessons selected by you in the **Prelaboratory Assignment** that you reviewed in this lab.

    2. List the lessons assigned by your instructor that you reviewed in this lab.

B. *Concentrated Chemical Concepts*

    1. List the lessons selected by you in the **Prelaboratory Assignment** that you reviewed in this lab.

    2. List the lessons assigned by your instructor that you reviewed in this lab.

C. *Exploring Chemistry*

    1. List the lessons selected by you in the **Prelaboratory Assignment** that you reviewed in this lab.

    2. List the lessons assigned by your instructor that you reviewed in this lab.

Questions

1. What are the advantages of using these interactive computer programs to study chemistry?

2. What are the disadvantages of using these interactive computer programs to study chemistry?

3. Write a brief assessment of your experience in the computer lab. Comment on what you liked and what you did not like about the lab. Comment on what you found helpful about the lab and what was not helpful.

Comprehensive Chemistry
Falcon Software

General Chemistry Topics

The following is a list of the lessons in this program that are appropriate and useful for Chemistry 100.

Elements

    The Periodic Table
    Names of the Elements
    Recognition of the Elements
    Isotopes and Atomic Weights
    Elements, Compounds, Mixtures

Metric System

    Prefixes
    Temperature
    Length
    Volume
    Mass
    Density

Nomenclature

    Binary Salts
    Variable Oxidation States
    Binary Nonmetals
    Acids
    Bases
    Ternary Salts
    Practice Problems

Empirical Formulas

    Percent Composition
    Empirical Formulas
    Mg-HCl Experiment
    Empirical Formula Problems

Atomic Weights

Chemical Formulas
Atomic Mass
Molecular and Formula Mass
Gram Molecular Weight
Gram-Mole Problems

Chemical Reactions

Writing Formulas
Chemical Reactions
Chemical Equations
Balancing Equations

Solutions and Solubility

Molarity
Dilutions
Ions in Solution
Net Ionic Equations
Solubility
Solubility Unknown
Three Beaker Unknown

Acids and Bases

Acids and Bases
Acid Base Reactions
Metal and Nonmetal Oxides
pH
pH Unknown
Weak Acids and Bases

Orbitals and Electrons

Orbitals and Electrons
Transition Metal Electrons

Concentrated Chemical Concepts
Trinity Software

General Chemistry Topics

The following is a list of the lessons in this program that are appropriate and useful for Chemistry 100.

Menu page 1

Definitions: Measurements
Common SI Prefixes
Significant Digits
Conversion of Units
Temperature Conversions
Density Problems
Definitions: Matter & Energy
Names & Symbols of Elements
Definitions: Atoms & Elements
Composition of Atoms

Menu page 2

Electron Configurations of Atoms
Elementary Electron Dot Structures
Areas of the Periodic Table
Definitions: Compounds & Moles
Names & Formulas of Simple Ions
Electron Configurations of Ions
Names & Formulas of Ionic Compounds
Names & Formulas of Polyatomic Ions
Balancing Chemical Reactions
Molar Masses (Formula Weights)

Menu page 3

Calculations with Moles
Definitions: Solutions & Colloids
Molarity Calculations
Definitions: Ion-Producing Substances
Names & Formulas of Acids and Bases

Menu page 4

    Names & Formulas of Conjugate Acids & Bases
    Strengths of Acids & Bases
    Solubilities of Salts
    Definitions: Acidity
    Values of pH

Menu page 5

    Stoichiometry Problems
    Names & Symbols of Essential Elements

Exploring Chemistry
Falcon Software

General Chemistry Topics

The following is a list of the lessons in this program that are
appropriate and useful for Chemistry 100.

Chemical Reactions

    Elements, Compounds, Mixtures
    Chemical Reactions
    Chemical Equations
    Balancing Equations

Solubility

    Ions in Solution
    Net Ionic Equations
    Solubility
    Solubility Unknowns
    Three Beaker Unknowns

Acids and Bases

    Acids and Bases
    Acid Base Reactions
    Metal and Nonmetal Oxides
    Weak Acids and Bases
    pH
    pH Unknowns

Orbitals and Electrons

    Orbitals and Electrons
    Transition Metal Electrons

PHYSICAL AND CHEMICAL CHANGES

Objective

The objective of this experiment is to learn how matter can be changed physically and chemically. You will make observations that allow you to distinguish between physical and chemical changes.

Introduction

A sample of matter can be classified according to the physical and chemical properties it exhibits. Changes in which the physical properties of a substance are altered are called physical changes, while changes in which chemical properties are altered are called chemical changes.

A physical change is one that alters a physical property of a substance without changing its chemical identity. Breaking a piece of glass into small pieces is an example of a physical change. The broken glass still has the same chemical composition and the same chemical properties as the original piece of glass, but the external form of the glass has changed. If liquid water is placed in a freezer, it will change to a solid in a process called freezing. This is another example of a physical change because only the state of the substance has changed. It is still water after it has solidified. Melting, which is the reverse of freezing, and evaporation, which involves a change from the liquid to the vapor state, are additional examples of physical changes.

As another example, consider what happens when table salt (sodium chloride, NaCl) is added to water and dissolved. After the salt has dissolved in the water, you no longer see the white, crystalline solid. However, a change in chemical composition has not occurred. The mixture still contains the water molecules, the sodium ions, and the chloride ions that were present in the original substances. The water and the salt are not converted to other types of substances when they are mixed together. This dissolving process is a physical change.

A characteristic of many physical changes is the fact that they can easily be reversed by changing the direction of heat flow. For example, liquid water can be converted to the solid state, or ice, by removing heat energy. This physical change, called freezing, can be reversed simply by adding heat energy to the ice. The original liquid water is obtained through melting of the ice. A useful characteristic of physical changes is that they can by employed to separate the components of a mixture. Consider a solution containing salt dissolved in water. This solution is a mixture. If the water is allowed to evaporate, the salt will remain behind as a solid. The water vapor can then be condensed back to liquid water. The components of the mixture can be separated and obtained in their original form by using the physical changes of evaporation and condensation.

Chemical changes are changes in which substances are transformed into new substances. For example, sodium, which is a soft, shiny metal, undergoes a chemical change when it is combined with water. The sodium and water react to produce sodium hydroxide and hydrogen gas. The heat produced in this reaction is often sufficient to cause the hydrogen to ignite and burn. This reactivity of sodium with water is a chemical property of the sodium. The change is a chemical change because the original substances, sodium and water, are transformed into new substances, sodium hydroxide and hydrogen.

As another example, consider what happens when sodium and chlorine, which is a green-yellow gas, are combined. When these substances come in contact, a rather incredible thing happens. Large amounts of heat and light energy are produced. When the reaction subsides, the sodium and chlorine are gone. They are replaced by an entirely new substance – the compound sodium chloride. The new compound has chemical properties that are entirely different from those of the substances from which it was made. For example, the sodium chloride does not react with water as sodium does. It is ordinary table salt. The process that occurs when sodium and chlorine are mixed is a chemical change.

In the laboratory, there are certain observations that can be made to determine whether a chemical change has occurred. Energy in the form of heat may be absorbed or released during a chemical change. This can produce a temperature change that might be observed by the sense of touch. Energy in the form of light is released in some chemical changes. This can be observed visually. The products of chemical changes are frequently gases or insoluble precipitates. Visual observation of the formation of bubbles or a solid in a reaction mixture might indicate that a chemical change is occurring. Finally, many chemicals have characteristic colors. Visually observed color changes may indicate chemical changes.

r group)

drops per group)

)

e gentle boiling for evaporating
h the silver nitrate solution.

idents work in groups of 2 or 3

o small pieces. Put the pieces
.

the   be strongly with a Bunsen burner for
several minutes. Record your observations.

B. Changes involving sand and sodium chloride

1. Measure out 0.50 g samples of sand and sodium chloride on
   different pieces of weighing paper.

2. Mix the two samples together in a 250-mL beaker. Add 50 mL
   of water and stir. Observe what happens to the sand and to
   the sodium chloride.

3. Set up a gravity filtration assembly as follows:

   a. Support a funnel on a ring stand using your iron ring
      and clay triangle.
   b. Fold a piece of filter paper in half, and then in
      quarters, producing a cone.
   c. Set the filter paper cone in the funnel with the tip of
      the cone fitted into the stem of the funnel.
   d. Holding the filter paper in place, wet it using
      distilled water from your water bottle. Pour out the
      excess water.

4. Filter the contents of the beaker from step 2 into a graduated cylinder. Record the volume of the filtrate collected (liquid that passed through the filter paper).

5. Equip a ring stand with an iron ring and wire screen for heating a beaker with your Bunsen burner.

6. Determine the mass of a clean, dry 250-mL beaker.

7. Add one half of your filtrate from step 4 to this beaker and record the volume of filtrate added. Save the other half portion of the filtrate for step 10.

8. Place the beaker on the ring stand and gently boil the filtrate until all the water evaporates and the remaining substance is completely dry. Then allow the beaker to cool.

9. Determine the mass of the beaker and the substance it contains. Calculate the mass and record the appearance of the substance remaining in the beaker.

10. Record the volume of the remaining portion of the filtrate from step 7 and pour it into a 100-mL beaker. Add 5 drops of 0.3 M silver nitrate solution to the beaker and stir. Record your observation.

11. Set up a filtration assembly as described in step 3 and filter the mixture from step 10.

12. When all the liquid has drained through the filter paper, remove the filter paper from the funnel and spread it out on a watch glass. Record the appearance of the substance on the filter paper being sure to note the color.

13. Place the watch glass and filter paper in a location on your lab bench where there is good exposure to the laboratory lights. Allow the material on the filter paper to be exposed to the light for about 15 minutes. Record the appearance of the substance after light exposure being sure to note the color.

CHEMICAL REACTIONS

Objective

In this experiment, you will visually observe the formation of a new substance as a result of a chemical reaction. You will isolate this new substance and quantitatively determine how much of it is produced in the reaction.

Introduction

A chemical reaction always involves the conversion of one or more substances, called reactants, into one or more different substances, called products. On the submicroscopic level, a reaction involves the regrouping of atoms or ions to form the new substances. When chemical reactions occur, there are frequently, but not always, changes that can be detected by your physical senses. In the laboratory, you can use your senses of sight, smell, and touch to determine when a chemical reaction occurs. For obvious safety reasons, you are not to use your sense of taste in the lab.

One of the ways you can sense that a chemical reaction has occurred is by observing the formation of a precipitate. A precipitate results when a product of the reaction is insoluble in the solvent being used. This insoluble product may consist of small particles that appear as a cloudy suspension or larger particles that rapidly settle to the bottom of the container. In describing a precipitate, you should always note its color.

A second way of determining that a reaction has occurred is by observing the formation of a gas. Gas evolution involves the formation of bubbles in the reaction mixture when a gaseous product is insoluble in the solvent. Gas evolution occurs in the decomposition of some unstable acids. For example, carbonic acid will form carbon dioxide and water on heating.

$$H_2CO_3(aq) \rightarrow CO_2(g) + H_2O(l)$$

Most gases are colorless and odorless. Some gases have distinctive odors, however, and the sense of smell can be used to identify them.

A third way of determining that a reaction has occurred is by observing a change in the color of the reaction mixture.

Color changes can be quite vivid, especially in oxidation-reduction reactions. In these reactions, one substance loses electrons and is oxidized, while a second substance gains electrons and is reduced.

A fourth way to observe that a chemical reaction has occurred is to detect a change in the temperature of the reaction mixture. When energy is released by the chemicals as a result of a chemical reaction, there is an increase in the temperature of the reaction mixture. Such a reaction is called exothermic. Combustion reactions are exothermic. For example, when methane is burned in a Bunsen burner, heat is produced.

$$CH_4(g) \ + \ 2 \ O_2(g) \ \rightarrow \ CO_2(g) \ + \ 2 \ H_2O(g) \ + \ heat$$

If energy is absorbed when a reaction occurs, the temperature of the reaction mixture will decrease. Such a reaction is called endothermic. The sense of touch can be used to determine whether a chemical reaction has occurred if sufficient energy is released or absorbed to produce a detectable temperature change. This is done by simply touching the container holding the reaction mixture to determine if it feels warmer or colder.

In general, a chemical reaction is described with a chemical equation. The chemical equation is a statement that represents the reacting species and those produced with formulas and symbols. A proper chemical equation is based on experimental evidence. Simply writing an equation does not mean that the reaction actually takes place. Also, to be in agreement with the Law of Conservation of Mass, the equation must be balanced. Only balanced equations can be used in chemical calculations.

In this experiment, you will observe the reaction that takes place when solutions of calcium chloride and sodium carbonate are mixed. The products are sodium chloride and calcium carbonate. Sodium chloride is soluble in water, and it will remain in solution. Calcium carbonate, however, is insoluble in water, and it will appear as a precipitate. This will be the visible sign that a chemical reaction has occurred. You will collect the calcium carbonate by filtration, dry it, and determine the mass and the number of moles of this product of the reaction.

Materials

0.2 M sodium carbonate (Na_2CO_3) (5 mL per student)
0.2 M calcium chloride ($CaCl_2$) (5 mL per student)

filter paper (1 piece per student)

Precautions

Be sure to clean up all spills immediately and to dispose of all waste and excess chemicals in the proper container. Never return excess chemicals to the reagent bottles.

Procedure

It is recommended that students work individually for this experiment.

1. Place 5 mL of 0.2 M sodium carbonate solution in a clean 25x200-mm test tube.

2. Carefully add 5 mL of 0.2 M calcium chloride solution to the test tube. Record your observation. Save your reaction mixture by placing the test tube in your test tube rack.

3. Set up a filtration assembly as follows:

   A. Place a clean funnel in a 250-mL Erlenmeyer flask.
   B. Write your initials on the edge of a piece of filter paper, and determine the mass of the filter paper.
   C. Fold the filter paper in half, and then in quarters, producing a cone.
   D. Set the filter paper cone in the funnel with the tip of the cone fitted into the stem of the funnel.
   E. Holding the filter paper in place, wet it using distilled water from your water bottle. Pour out the excess water.

4. Carefully pour the contents of your test tube from step 2 into the funnel. Do not fill the filter paper cone higher than 1/8 inch from the top of the paper.

5. To make sure that all the solid in your reaction mixture is transferred, rinse the test tube two or three times with small portions of distilled water, and transfer the rinse water to the funnel.

6. After all of the liquid has drained into the Erlenmeyer flask, carefully remove the filter paper and its contents from the funnel. Spread out the filter paper on a watch glass.

7. The solid on the filter paper is the calcium carbonate precipitate that was formed in your reaction. Dry the filter paper and this precipitate on the watch glass in the oven.

8. Determine the mass of the dried filter paper with the dried precipitate on it.

9. Calculate the mass and the number of moles of calcium carbonate produced in your reaction.

CHEMICAL REACTIONS

Name _____

Date _____

Prelaboratory Assignment

1. How is a chemical change distinguished from a physical change?

2. List four kinds of observations that can lead you to conclude that a chemical reaction has occurred.

3. How small of a change in temperature do you think you can detect by your sense of touch? How could smaller changes in temperature be detected?

CHEMICAL REACTIONS

Name _____

Date _____

Laboratory Report

Results

1. Volume of sodium carbonate solution _____

2. Volume of calcium chloride solution _____

3. Record your observation on mixing these two solutions.

4. Mass of filter paper _____

5. Mass of dried filter paper and calcium carbonate _____

6. Mass of calcium carbonate _____

7. Calculate the number of moles of calcium carbonate produced in your reaction. Show your work.

8. Write a balanced chemical equation for the chemical reaction that took place in this experiment.

Questions

1. Balance the following chemical equations.

   A. __ Mg(s) + __ HCl(aq) → __ $MgCl_2$(aq) + __ H_2(g)

   B. __NaHCO$_3$(s) + __HCl(aq) → __NaCl(aq) + __H_2O(l) + __CO_2(g)

   C. __NaHSO$_3$(s) + __HCl(aq) → __NaCl(aq) + __H_2O(l) + __SO_2(g)

   D. __ FeS(s) + __ HCl(aq) → __ $FeCl_2$(aq) + __ H_2S(g)

   E. __ $BaCl_2$(aq) + __ Na_2SO_4(aq) → __ NaCl(aq) + __ $BaSO_4$(s)

   F. __ Mg(s) + __ O_2(g) → __ MgO(s)

2. For each of the chemical equations in question 1, describe observations that you might make in the laboratory to determine that the chemical reaction actually occurs.

   A.

   B.

   C.

   D.

   E.

   F.

REACTIVITIES OF METALS

Objective

Your objective in this experiment is to investigate the chemical reactivities of several common metals. By observing reactions of these metals with various test reagents, you will be able to rank the metals from most reactive to least reactive.

Introduction

The metallic elements exhibit a wide range of chemical reactivities from highly active metals such as sodium and potassium, which react vigorously with many substances, to metals of low activity such as gold and platinum. In many of their reactions, metals displace less active elements from compounds. For example, aluminum reacts with nitric acid and with silver nitrate according to the following chemical equations, which show aluminum displacing less active hydrogen and silver from their compounds.

$$2 \ Al(s) \ + \ 6 \ HNO_3(aq) \ \rightarrow \ 2 \ Al(NO_3)_3(aq) \ + \ 3 \ H_2(g)$$
$$Al(s) \ + \ 3 \ AgNO_3(aq) \ \rightarrow \ Al(NO_3)_3(aq) \ + \ 3 \ Ag(s)$$

Metal atoms lose electrons in displacement reactions to form cations. For example, Al atoms form Al^{3+} cations in the above equations. The rate and vigor of each reaction will depend to a large extent on the inherent reactivity of the metal. Other factors such as temperature, concentration, and metal particle size also affect reaction rate.

In this experiment, you will investigate reactions of the metals calcium, copper, iron, lead, magnesium, and zinc with water, hydrochloric acid, and copper(II) nitrate solution. The reactions, if they occur, will be displacement reactions as described above. Production of gas bubbles, a color change, precipitate formation, formation of a metallic coating on the reacting metal, and heat generation are observable signs that a chemical reaction is occurring. Only very active metals will react with water, while metals of lower activity will react with hydrochloric acid. Also, any metal that is more active than copper will displace copper from copper(II) nitrate. By observing which reactions occur and which do not, and by observing the relative rates of the reactions, you will be able to determine the order of reactivity of the metals.

Materials

calcium (1-2 small pieces per group)
copper, iron, lead, magnesium, zinc (6-8 pieces each per group)

6 M hydrochloric acid (5 mL per group)
0.1 M copper(II) nitrate (15 mL per group)
distilled water (18 mL per group)

Precautions

Do not touch the calcium or lead samples with your bare hands. Handle the hydrochloric acid carefully. Dispose of the chemicals (especially the lead) in the proper waste container.

Procedure

It is recommended that students work in groups of 2 or 3 for this experiment.

A. Reactions with water

1. Place approximately equal amounts of calcium, copper, iron, lead, magnesium, and zinc into separate, labeled 16x150-mm test tubes, one metal sample per test tube. In most cases, 3 or 4 small pieces of the metal sample will be sufficient. Only use 1 or 2 small pieces of calcium.

2. Add 3 mL of distilled water to each test tube and record your initial observations on any signs of reaction.

3. Allow the test tubes to stand for 5 minutes. Record your final observations on signs of reaction.

B. Reactions with hydrochloric acid

1. Add 1 mL of 6 M hydrochloric acid to each of the test tubes above, except for the one that contains the calcium sample. Gently shake each test tube.

2. Allow the test tubes to stand for 5 minutes. Record your observations on signs of reaction, paying close attention to gas formation and heat generation. Indicate the relative rate, or vigor, of each reaction.

3. After recording your observations, dispose of all the samples in the proper waste container.

C. Reactions with copper(II) nitrate

1. Place approximately equal amounts of copper, iron, lead, magnesium, and zinc (omit calcium) into separate, labeled 16x150-mm test tubes, one metal sample per test tube. In most cases, 3 or 4 small pieces of the metal sample will be sufficient.

2. Add 3 mL of 0.1 M copper(II) nitrate solution to each test tube.

3. Allow the test tubes to stand for 10 minutes. Record your observations on signs of reaction, paying close attention to color changes in the copper(II) nitrate solutions.

4. Carefully pour the solution out of each test tube being sure that you do not lose the metal sample.

5. Dump the metal samples onto a paper towel so that you can examine them. Record your observations, paying close attention to any metallic coatings that may have formed on the pieces of metal.

6. After recording your observations, scrape the pieces of metal off of the paper towel and into the waste container.

THE MOLE CONCEPT

Objective

This experiment is designed to help you understand the concept of the mole. You will measure out and compare samples consisting of one mole each of three different substances.

Introduction

Atoms and molecules have such small masses and sizes that chemists are seldom able to deal with them one at a time. When a chemist measures out even very small quantities of substances, huge numbers of atoms and molecules are present. To effectively deal with this problem of handling very large numbers of very small objects, chemists have defined a unit called the mole.

One mole of any compound has a mass equal to the formula mass of the compound expressed in grams. For instance, the formula mass of CO_2 is 44.0 amu (12.0 + 16.0 + 16.0 = 44.0). Therefore, one mole of CO_2 is 44.0 grams of CO_2. Likewise, the formula mass of $(NH_2)_2CO$ is 60.0 amu, and one mole of $(NH_2)_2CO$ is 60.0 grams of this compound. For an element, one mole has a mass equal to the atomic mass of the element in grams. For the elements C and Fe, the atomic masses are 12.0 amu and 55.8 amu, respectively. Therefore, one mole of C is 12.0 grams of C, and one mole of Fe is 55.8 grams of Fe.

Chemists have determined experimentally that one mole of any compound contains 6.02×10^{23} molecules of that compound. In other words, 44.0 grams of CO_2 contain 6.02×10^{23} CO_2 molecules, and 60.0 grams of $(NH_2)_2CO$, likewise, contain 6.02×10^{23} $(NH_2)_2CO$ molecules. Similarly, one mole of an element contains 6.02×10^{23} atoms of that element. Thus, 12.0 grams of C contain 6.02×10^{23} C atoms, while 55.8 grams of Fe contain 6.02×10^{23} Fe atoms. We can therefore say, as a secondary definition, that a mole is 6.02×10^{23} units of something. As you can see from this secondary definition, there is nothing mysterious about the mole concept. Just as we call 12 of anything a dozen and 20 a score, we call 6.02×10^{23} units a mole. The number 6.02×10^{23} is called Avogadro's number, after the Italian scientist Amedeo Avogadro (1776-1856).

In conclusion, samples consisting of one mole each of different substances will contain equal numbers of atoms or molecules, but the samples will have different masses because of the different formula masses of the substances. A summary of this information for the four substances that were discussed above is given here.

1 mole CO_2 = 6.02 x 10^{23} CO_2 molecules = 44.0 g CO_2
1 mole $(NH_2)_2CO$ = 6.02 x 10^{23} $(NH_2)_2CO$ molecules = 60.0 g $(NH_2)_2CO$
1 mole C = 6.02 x 10^{23} C atoms = 12.0 g C
1 mole Fe = 6.02 x 10^{23} Fe atoms = 55.8 g Fe

Materials

distilled water (H_2O)
sodium chloride (NaCl)
aluminum (Al)

Precautions

Use normal laboratory precautions. Since the chemical samples are used only for observational purposes, the sodium chloride and the aluminum do not need to be disposed of in a waste container. These samples may be returned to their original containers.

Procedure

It is recommended that students work in groups of 2 or 3 for this experiment.

1. Determine the mass of a 50-mL graduated cylinder. Add one mole of distilled water to the graduated cylinder. What mass of distilled water did you add to the graduated cylinder? Record the volume of the sample. Record the number of molecules in the sample.

2. Determine the mass of a 250-mL beaker. Add one mole of sodium chloride to the beaker. What mass of sodium chloride did you add to the beaker? Record the number of formula units in the sample.

3. Determine the mass of a 250-mL beaker. Add one mole of aluminum to the beaker. What mass of aluminum did you add to the beaker? Record the number of atoms in the sample.

4. Summarize and compare your results from steps 1, 2, and 3 by completing the table in section D of the laboratory report.

FORMULA OF A HYDRATE

Objective

Your objective in this lab is to determine experimentally the formula of a copper(II) sulfate hydrate unknown. You will accomplish this by determining the ratio of the moles of products obtained in the thermal decomposition of the hydrate.

Introduction

Many ionic compounds that have been crystallized from aqueous solution appear to be perfectly dry. Yet when heated, they yield large quantities of water in the form of steam. The ionic crystals usually change in form, and sometimes in color, as the water is driven off, indicating that the water was present as an integral part of the crystal structure. Such compounds are called hydrates. When the water is driven out of the hydrate, the resulting compound is said to be anhydrous (without water).

An example of a hydrate is magnesium sulfate heptahydrate, $MgSO_4 \cdot 7H_2O$, where the centered dot ($\cdot$) is a special notation used to designate water of hydration. This formula indicates that the hydrate contains H_2O and $MgSO_4$ in a 7-to-1 mole ratio. Thermal decomposition of this hydrate is described by the following chemical equation. This balanced equation shows that the

$$MgSO_4 \cdot 7H_2O(s) \xrightarrow{\Delta} MgSO_4(s) + 7\ H_2O(g)$$

decomposition products, H_2O and $MgSO_4$, are formed in a 7-to-1 mole ratio. Both the hydrate formula and the balanced equation for its decomposition give the same ratio of the moles of H_2O to the moles of $MgSO_4$, namely moles H_2O/moles $MgSO_4 = 7/1 = 7$. This correlation is the basis of the procedure used in this lab for determining the formula of the unknown hydrate.

In this experiment, you will analyze a copper(II) sulfate hydrate unknown, $CuSO_4 \cdot nH_2O$, in order to determine its formula by finding the value of n. You will thermally decompose the hydrate by heating a sample of known mass in a crucible. If sufficient heat is added, all of the hydrate will decompose to anhydrous copper(II) sulfate and water as shown in the following equation.

$$CuSO_4 \cdot nH_2O(s) \xrightarrow{\Delta} CuSO_4(s) + n\ H_2O(g)$$

The anhydrous copper(II) sulfate will remain in the crucible as a solid residue, while the water will be driven away as steam under the high-temperature reaction conditions. According to the Law of Conservation of Mass, the difference between the masses of copper(II) sulfate hydrate and anhydrous copper(II) sulfate will equal the mass of the water lost during the reaction. The masses of anhydrous copper(II) sulfate and water can be converted into moles using the respective molar masses. The ratio of the moles of these products will then establish the value of n in the hydrate formula $CuSO_4 \cdot nH_2O$. That is, moles H_2O/moles $CuSO_4$ = n/1 = n.

Materials

copper(II) sulfate hydrate (4-5 g per student)

Precautions

The crucible, iron ring, and Bunsen burner will get very hot during the heating process. Handle these objects carefully in order to avoid burns. Also, do not place a hot crucible on the balance. Allow it to cool before determining its mass.

Procedure

It is recommended that students work individually for this experiment.

1. Equip a ring stand with an iron ring and a clay triangle.

2. Place a clean, dry, covered crucible in the clay triangle and heat it with a Bunsen burner for 5 minutes. The burner should be adjusted to give a blue, non-luminous flame. The tip of the inner flame cone is the hottest part of the flame and should just touch the bottom of the crucible.

3. Remove the hot crucible from the clay triangle using tongs and allow it to cool on a wire screen. Determine the mass of the covered crucible to the nearest 0.01 g.

4. Place enough copper(II) sulfate hydrate in the crucible to fill it approximately 1/3 to 1/2 full. Observe the physical appearance of the hydrate sample (color, size and shape of crystals, etc.). Replace the crucible cover. Determine the mass of the covered crucible and hydrate sample to the nearest 0.01 g.

5. Calculate the mass of the hydrate sample.

6. Place the covered crucible in the clay triangle and heat gently for 5 minutes. The burner should be adjusted so that the tip of the inner flame cone is about 1 inch from the bottom of the crucible.

7. After this initial gently heating, adjust the burner so that the tip of the inner flame cone just touches the bottom of the crucible. Heat strongly for 10 minutes. If the sample starts to smoke, reduce the heat.

8. Remove the hot crucible from the clay triangle and allow it to cool on the wire screen. Be sure to keep the crucible covered during the cooling period. Determine the mass of the covered crucible and anhydrous residue to the nearest 0.01 g.

9. Replace the covered crucible in the clay triangle and heat strongly for another 10 minutes. Allow the crucible to cool and again determine the mass of the covered crucible and anhydrous residue. If this mass and the mass in step 8 differ by 0.02 g or less, proceed to step 10. If the mass difference is greater than 0.02 g, consult your instructor about the necessity of a third heating.

10. Using the result of the final heating, calculate the mass of the anhydrous residue that remains in the crucible. Using the mass of the hydrate sample and the mass of the anhydrous residue, calculate the mass of the water that was in the original hydrate sample.

11. Observe the physical appearance of the anhydrous copper(II) sulfate. Observe what happens when 5 drops of water are added to this anhydrous residue.

12. Dispose of all waste chemicals in the proper waste container.

13. Determine the formula of the hydrate unknown.

EMPIRICAL FORMULA DETERMINATION

Objective

In this lab, you will determine the simplest formula of a compound – that is, its empirical formula. To do this, you will measure the mass of each element that is present in a sample of the compound that you prepare.

Introduction

The composition of a chemical compound is independent of its source, provided it has been purified and separated from all other substances. The composition can be determined by chemically breaking the compound into its component elements. These same elements can be recombined in the proper proportions, as dictated by the composition of the compound, to produce the original compound again. These facts are summarized by the Law of Definite Proportions: When elements chemically combine to form a compound, they do so in a definite proportion by mass. The composition of a compound can be used to determine the simplest, or empirical, formula of that compound.

In this experiment, a sample of magnesium chloride will be prepared by reacting a known mass of magnesium with an excess of hydrochloric acid. From the masses of the magnesium used and the magnesium chloride produced, the mass of chlorine in the sample can be determined. The moles of magnesium and moles of chlorine that are present in the sample can then be calculated from the respective masses as shown below.

$$\text{moles of Mg} = \text{mass of Mg} \times \frac{1 \text{ mole Mg}}{24.3 \text{ g Mg}}$$

$$\text{moles of Cl} = \text{mass of Cl} \times \frac{1 \text{ mole Cl}}{35.5 \text{ g Cl}}$$

The ratio of the moles of magnesium to the moles of chlorine can then be calculated and converted to the smallest whole number ratio of moles. This will determine the subscripts of Mg and Cl in the empirical formula of the magnesium chloride.

Materials

magnesium (Mg) (1 strip per group)

1.0 M hydrochloric acid (HCl(aq)) (50 mL per group)

evaporating dish (1 per group)

Precautions

Hydrochloric acid is corrosive and can cause severe skin burns. If it comes in contact with your skin, immediately wash the affected area with large quantities of water and notify your instructor. Take care when handling hot objects.

Procedure

It is recommended that students work in groups of 2 or 3 for this experiment.

1. Determine the mass of a clean, dry evaporating dish.

2. Determine the mass of a strip of magnesium. Then place the magnesium in the evaporating dish.

3. In the fume hood, slowly add 50 mL of 1.0 M hydrochloric acid to the evaporating dish. Record your observations.

4. Allow the reaction to continue, still in the fume hood, until no more magnesium is visible.

5. Place the evaporating dish on a hot plate in the fume hood. Adjust the hot plate so that the reaction mixture boils gently. Allow the mixture to boil to dryness. The material remaining in the evaporating dish is magnesium chloride. It may not be completely dry, however.

6. Cool the evaporating dish to room temperature. Describe the appearance of the magnesium chloride.

7. Determine the mass of the evaporating dish and the magnesium chloride.

8. In the laboratory, set up a ring stand with an iron ring and wire screen. Place the evaporating dish on the wire screen, and heat it for three minutes using a Bunsen burner. Allow the evaporating dish to cool to room temperature.

9. Re-determine the mass of the evaporating dish and the magnesium chloride. If the mass loss since the previous determination exceeds 0.05 g, the magnesium chloride was not completely dried in step 5. The heating process should be repeated until the mass loss after successive heatings is less than 0.05 g. At this point, the magnesium chloride will be thoroughly dried.

10. Calculate the mass of chlorine in the magnesium chloride.

EMPIRICAL FORMULA
DETERMINATION

Name _____

Date _____

Prelaboratory Assignment

1. A. What is the charge of the ion that a magnesium atom will usually form?

   B. What is the charge of the ion that a chlorine atom will usually form?

   C. What is the correct formula for magnesium chloride?

   D. What is the accepted mole ratio of magnesium to chlorine in magnesium chloride?

2. Determine the empirical formula of a compound which has a percent composition of 40.04% S and 59.96% O. Show all of your calculations.

EMPIRICAL FORMULA DETERMINATION

Name _____

Date _____

Laboratory Report

Results

A. Experimental measurements and observations

1. Mass of evaporating dish _____

2. Mass of magnesium strip (Mg) _____

3. Volume of 1.0 M hydrochloric acid used _____

4. Record your observations on adding the hydrochloric acid to the magnesium.

5. Describe the appearance of the magnesium chloride.

6. Mass of evaporating dish and magnesium chloride _____
   (after boiling to dryness on hot plate)

7. Mass of evaporating dish and magnesium chloride _____
   (after first heating with Bunsen burner)

8. Mass of evaporating dish and magnesium chloride _____
   (after second heating, if necessary)

9. Mass of chlorine (Cl) in the magnesium chloride _____

B. Calculations

1. Moles of magnesium (show calculation)   _____

   moles of Mg = mass of Mg x (1 mole Mg/24.3 g Mg)

2. Moles of chlorine (show calculation)   _____

   moles of Cl = mass of Cl x (1 mole Cl/35.5 g Cl)

3. Smaller number of moles   _____

4. Mole ratio of magnesium to chlorine

   a. Moles of Mg/smaller number of moles   _____

   b. Moles of Cl/smaller number of moles   _____

   c. Smallest whole number ratio of a to b   _____

5. Empirical formula of magnesium chloride   _____

Questions

1. Write a balanced chemical equation for the reaction of magnesium and hydrochloric acid.

2. How many moles and how many grams of magnesium chloride can be formed from 2.5 moles of magnesium?

3. In this experiment, how would your determination of the empirical formula be affected if the magnesium chloride product was not completely dried?

OXYGEN – A MICROSCALE EXPERIMENT

Objective

Your objective in this experiment is to prepare oxygen gas and observe some of its properties. In order to become familiar with a new laboratory method, you will follow a procedure that makes use of microscale techniques.

Introduction

Oxygen is a very abundant element that is essential for life on earth. It exists in the free state as a diatomic molecule, O_2, and is a gas at room temperature and pressure. There are a number of different methods that can be used to prepare oxygen in the laboratory, and some of its properties are fairly easy to determine. This experiment will employ microscale techniques to prepare and study the oxygen. These techniques involve the use of small-scale equipment and small amounts of chemicals. Microscale work is economical in terms of the reagents being used and waste disposal, and it provides an added level of safety compared to traditional lab techniques.

Small amounts of oxygen gas can be prepared in the laboratory by decomposing certain oxygen-containing compounds. In this experiment, you will use the decomposition of hydrogen peroxide. In the presence of the catalyst manganese(IV) oxide, hydrogen peroxide decomposes at room temperature according to the following chemical equation.

$$2\ H_2O_2\,(aq) \xrightarrow{\ MnO_2\ } 2\ H_2O\,(l)\ +\ O_2\,(g)$$

The rate of this catalyzed decomposition is such that the oxygen can conveniently be collected by displacement of water.

Oxygen gas has certain chemical and physical properties that can easily be studied in the laboratory. For example, oxygen is necessary for combustion. In order to burn a piece of wood, oxygen must be present; the greater the concentration of the oxygen, the faster the wood will burn. The fact that oxygen is needed for combustion is a chemical property of the oxygen. The effect that the concentration of oxygen has on the rate of combustion is the basis for the "glowing splint" test for detecting oxygen. You will investigate this test in this experiment.

A physical property of oxygen is its density, which is mass per unit volume. It is fairly easy to determine the relative densities of gases. Consider the fact that a helium-filled balloon will rise, or float, when it is released in the air. This occurs because helium gas is less dense than air. In this experiment, you will determine the density of oxygen gas relative to the density of air.

When chemical substances react, they do so in certain fixed proportions. For example, when carbon is burned to form carbon dioxide, 1 mole of carbon will react and chemically combine with 1 mole of oxygen. In terms of masses, this amounts to 12.0 grams of carbon reacting with 32.0 grams of oxygen. Therefore, when any given amount of carbon is burned to form carbon dioxide, the amount of oxygen that is required is determined by the 1 mole O_2/1 mole C and the 32.0 g O_2/12.0 g C ratios.

In this lab, you will investigate the reaction of hydrogen and oxygen gases in order to determine the proportion in which they react. Hydrogen gas can be produced by reacting zinc with hydrochloric acid.

$$Zn(s) \; + \; 2 \, HCl(aq) \; \rightarrow \; ZnCl_2(aq) \; + \; H_2(g)$$

You will prepare and ignite mixtures containing various volumes of hydrogen and oxygen. Your observations will allow you to determine the fixed proportion in which the hydrogen and oxygen react. To interpret your results, it is helpful to know that the volume of a gas is directly proportional to the number of moles of the gas at constant temperature and pressure.

Materials

6% hydrogen peroxide solution ($H_2O_2(aq)$) (10 mL per group)
6.0 M hydrochloric acid (HCl(aq)) (10 mL per group)

manganese(IV) oxide (MnO_2) (0.1 g per group)
granular zinc (Zn) (1 g per group)

13x100-mm test tubes (2 per group)
gas-delivery stoppers (2 per group)
Beral pipet bulbs (3 per group)
pipet bulb holders (1 per group)
micro-spatulas (1 per group)
toothpicks (2-3 per group)
black markers (1 per 2-3 groups)

Precautions

Be sure to wear safety goggles. Do not allow the hydrogen peroxide or the hydrochloric acid to contact your skin. If skin contact does occur, immediately wash the affected area with soap and water. Always position your Bunsen burner away from the gas-generating units. Follow the directions exactly.

Procedure

It is recommended that students work in groups of 2 or 3 for this experiment.

A. Preparation and collection of oxygen gas

1. Completely fill 3 Beral pipet bulbs with distilled water using your water bottle. These will be used to collect the oxygen gas by displacement of the water. Store the filled bulbs with the openings pointing upward in the bulb holder.

2. Mark "O_2" as a label on a 13x100-mm test tube and fill it 3/4 full with 6% hydrogen peroxide. Using the tip of a micro-spatula, add a very small amount of manganese(IV) oxide to the tube. Observe the test tube immediately after addition of the manganese(IV) oxide.

3. Place a gas-delivery stopper in the mouth of the test tube and allow the reaction to proceed for 5 seconds to flush air from the system. This oxygen-generating unit can be held upright in a 100-mL beaker. Pack the extra space in the beaker with a paper towel to secure the test tube.

4. Place the opening of one of the water-filled pipet bulbs over the top of the gas-delivery stopper and begin to collect oxygen gas. Do not squeeze the bulb as this will force water out of it. Be certain to allow all of the water to be displaced by the oxygen. Store the gas-filled bulb with the opening pointing upward in the bulb holder.

B. Test for oxygen gas – the "glowing splint" test

1. Light your Bunsen burner and position it away from the oxygen-generating unit.

2. Ignite a toothpick using the burner. Gently blow out the toothpick's flame so that only a glowing ember remains.

3. Holding the oxygen-filled pipet bulb horizontally, quickly insert the glowing toothpick into the oxygen. Record your observations.

4. Turn off the Bunsen burner.

C. Relative densities of oxygen and air

1. Using the remaining water-filled pipet bulbs, collect 2 more samples of oxygen as described in step 4 of part A.

2. Simultaneously hold one of these oxygen-filled bulbs with the opening pointing upward and one with the opening pointing downward for a period of 5 minutes. Make certain that no water blocks the openings of the bulbs and do not squeeze them.

3. After 5 minutes, test each of the pipet bulbs for the presence of oxygen using a glowing toothpick as described in part B. Record your observations.

D. Reaction of hydrogen and oxygen gases

1. Using a black marker, draw lines on your 3 pipet bulbs dividing each bulb into 6 sections of equal volume. This will allow you to mix different volumes of hydrogen and oxygen gases. Also, number the bulbs 1 through 3.

2. Completely fill the 3 pipet bulbs with distilled water and store them in the bulb holder.

3. Mark "H_2" as a label on a second 13x100-mm test tube and fill it 3/4 full with 6.0 M hydrochloric acid. Using a micro-spatula, add a small amount of granular zinc to the tube. Observe the test tube after addition of the zinc.

4. Place a gas-delivery stopper in the mouth of the test tube and allow the reaction to proceed for 5 seconds to flush air from the system. This hydrogen-generating unit can be held upright in a 100-mL beaker. Pack the extra space in the beaker with a paper towel to secure the test tube. Do not have any open flames in the vicinity of the hydrogen-generating unit.

5. Examine the oxygen-generating unit that was assembled in part A. If there is no bubbling action in the reaction mixture, the hydrogen peroxide has been completely decomposed and oxygen gas is no longer being produced. If this is the case, dispose of the reaction mixture in the waste container and recharge the unit as described in steps 2 and 3 of part A. If there is sufficient bubbling, do not recharge the unit.

6. Prepare mixtures of hydrogen and oxygen by collecting samples of both gases in each of the water-filled pipet bulbs from step 2. The graduations on the bulbs allow you to collect and mix different volumes of these gases. Allow a small amount of water to remain in each of the bulbs to act as a seal. Store the gas-filled bulbs with the openings pointing downward in the bulb holder.

   a. In bulb 1, collect 1 volume of hydrogen and 5 volumes of oxygen.
   b. In bulb 2, collect 2 volumes of hydrogen and 4 volumes of oxygen.
   c. In bulb 3, collect 4 volumes of hydrogen and 2 volumes of oxygen.

7. Light your Bunsen burner and position it away from the gas-generating units.

8. Test the reactivity of each of the gas mixtures by igniting each mixture in the burner flame. Bring each gas-filled pipet bulb up to the burner, hold the opening of the bulb approximately 2 centimeters from the flame, and quickly squeeze the bulb. Record your observations paying close attention to the sound produced in each case. Rate the "pops" that you hear as loud, moderate, or soft.

OXYGEN – A MICROSCALE EXPERIMENT

Name _____

Date _____

Prelaboratory Assignment

1. In this lab, you will use the catalyst manganese(IV) oxide. Explain what a catalyst is.

2. A. Write a balanced chemical equation for the combustion, or burning, of carbon.

   B. Write a balanced chemical equation for the combustion of methane, CH_4.

3. If an iron nail is placed in a glass of water, the nail will sink. Is the density of iron smaller than or larger than the density of water? Explain.

4. Consider the reaction of nitrogen and hydrogen to form ammonia.

$$N_2 + 3 H_2 \rightarrow 2 NH_3$$

   A. How many moles of H_2 are needed to react with 1 mole of N_2?

   B. How many grams of H_2 are needed to react with 28.0 grams of N_2?

OXYGEN – A MICROSCALE EXPERIMENT

Name _____

Date _____

Laboratory Report

Results

A. Preparation and collection of oxygen gas

   Observations on adding manganese(IV) oxide to hydrogen peroxide:

B. Test for oxygen gas – the "glowing splint" test

   Observations on inserting a glowing toothpick into a sample of oxygen:

C. Relative densities of oxygen and air

   Results of "glowing splint" test on pipet bulb held upward:

   Results of "glowing splint" test on pipet bulb held downward:

D. Reaction of hydrogen and oxygen gases

Observations on adding zinc to hydrochloric acid:

Observations on igniting the hydrogen-oxygen mixtures:

Mixture	Volume ratio of gases	Observations; rate pops
1	1 vol. H_2/5 vol. O_2	
2	2 vol. H_2/4 vol. O_2	
3	4 vol. H_2/2 vol. O_2	

Questions

1. How do your observations in part A demonstrate the action of a catalyst?

2. A. Describe the procedure for the "glowing splint" test.

   B. Describe the positive result in this test that indicates the presence of oxygen.

3. Based on your observations in part C, is the density of oxygen smaller than or larger than the density of air? Explain your reasoning.

4. A. Based on your observations in part D, what is the optimum volume ratio of hydrogen to oxygen for their reaction? What is your basis for making this choice?

   B. Considering your answer in question A, what is the simplest, or smallest, optimum volume ratio of hydrogen to oxygen for their reaction?

   C. The volume of a gas is directly to the number of moles of the gas at constant temperature and pressure. Using this fact and your answer to question B, what is the optimum mole ratio of hydrogen to oxygen for their reaction?

   D. Write a balanced chemical equation for the reaction of hydrogen and oxygen. Using this equation, justify your answer for question C.

LABORATORY CHECK-OUT

Objective

Your objective is to ensure that the lab is left in a clean, orderly condition after completing your final experiment. You will inventory your equipment and clean your work area.

Introduction

By the time that students complete the final experiment of the course, their work areas undoubtedly will be dirty, and they probably will have missing or broken equipment. It is important, therefore, that students clean their work areas and inventory their equipment in order to leave the laboratory in a clean, orderly condition. This is a courtesy to subsequent users of the lab, and it is also a matter of safety.

Procedure

1. Check off each item on the **Check-Out List** as you complete the following steps of the procedure.

2. Remove the contents of your locker, placing all the items on the lab bench.

3. Using your towel, wipe out your locker before replacing any equipment.

4. Using the **CHEMISTRY LOCKER INVENTORY** sheet, make an inventory of your equipment. Return each item to your locker as you check it off the list. Be sure to wash and dry any dirty glassware. Replace any broken or missing items with equipment from the lab supply cabinet. Return extra items and any equipment not on the inventory list to the place indicated by your instructor.

5. Using your towel, wipe off your lab bench and clean around your balance. Remove any debris from your sink.

6. Place your dirty towel in the dirty-towel box.

7. After completing all of the above steps, have your instructor inspect your locker and work area. If all is satisfactory, your instructor will initial your **Check-Out List**.

LABORATORY CHECK-OUT

Name _____

Date _____

Check-Out List

1. Locker   _____ cleaned

2. Equipment   _____ cleaned

                   _____ broken and missing equipment replaced

                   _____ extra equipment returned

                   _____ inventory completed

3. Work area   _____ lab bench cleaned

                   _____ balance area cleaned

                   _____ sink cleaned

4. Instructor   _____
   initials

CHEMISTRY LOCKER INVENTORY

1 – apron or lab coat	1 – iron ring
1 – beaker, 100-mL	2 – medicine droppers
1 – beaker, 250-mL	1 – mortar and pestle
1 – beaker, 400-mL	4 – rubber stoppers, size 0
1 – beaker, 600-mL	1 – scoop
1 – Bunsen burner with tubing	1 – stirring rod
1 – clamp	1 – test tube holder
1 – clay triangle	1 – test tube rack
1 – crucible with cover	9 – test tubes, 16x150-mm
1 – Erlenmeyer flask, 50-mL	3 – test tubes, 25x200-mm
1 – Erlenmeyer flask, 125-mL	1 – tongs
1 – Erlenmeyer flask, 250-mL	1 – towel
1 – funnel	1 – watch glass
1 – graduated cylinder, 10-mL	1 – water bottle
1 – graduated cylinder, 50-mL	1 – wax pencil
1 – graduated cylinder, 100-mL	1 – wire screen

LECTURE SUPPLEMENT

COURSE OBJECTIVES

UNIT I: MEASUREMENT OF MATTER

After completing this unit, students should be able to:

1. State metric units and their abbreviations for length, mass, time, area, volume, density, heat, and temperature.

2. Give numerical values for common metric prefixes such as kilo-, centi-, milli-, and micro-.

3. Perform measurements in the laboratory using a meter stick, graduated cylinder, and balance.

4. Solve a variety of unit conversion problems (metric-metric, metric-English, etc.) using the conversion factor method.

5. Define density and explain its significance as a physical property used to help identify samples of matter.

6. Perform a variety of density calculations.

7. Explain how a liquid-in-glass thermometer works and how it can be calibrated using freezing and boiling water.

8. Solve a variety of temperature conversion problems involving the Celsius, Kelvin, and Fahrenheit scales.

9. Give numerical values for the freezing point, boiling point, and density of water.

10. Explain the concept of significant figures and determine the number of significant figures in a given measurement.

11. Round calculated quantities to the correct number of significant figures.

12. Express numbers using scientific notation and perform calculations with numbers written in scientific notation.

13. Use reference books (*Handbook of Chemistry and Physics*, *Merck Index*, etc.) to obtain data such as densities, solubilities, melting points, and boiling points.

14. Display data in graphical form.

UNIT II: PROPERTIES, CHANGES, AND CLASSIFICATION OF MATTER

After completing this unit, students should be able to:

1. Explain the differences between physical properties and chemical properties of matter and classify given properties as physical or chemical.

2. Use given properties to identify samples of matter.

3. Describe the differences between physical changes and chemical changes of matter and classify given changes as physical or chemical.

4. Draw pictures illustrating melting and boiling at the submicroscopic level.

5. Explain how heat energy is involved in various physical and chemical changes.

6. State characteristics of pure substances, mixtures, elements, and compounds and describe the classification of matter scheme.

7. Identify given samples of matter as pure substances or mixtures, as elements or compounds.

8. List general properties of metals and nonmetals.

UNIT III: STRUCTURE OF MATTER

After completing this unit, students should be able to:

1. Explain the basic ideas of the atomic theory of matter.

2. Write names and chemical symbols for selected elements.

3. State the charge and mass of each of the three fundamental subatomic particles that make up atoms.

4. Describe the Rutherford, or nuclear, model of the atom.

5. Define the terms atomic number, mass number, isotope, atomic mass, and ion and write nuclide symbols for various isotopes and ions.

6. Describe the electronic structure of atoms in terms of orbitals, subshells, and shells.

7. Write complete ground state electron configurations for atoms.

8. Determine the valence shell number and the number of valence electrons for an atom from its electron configuration and draw a Lewis dot symbol for the atom.

9. Explain the periodic system of classification of the elements.

10. Use the Periodic Chart to determine the atomic number and atomic mass of a given element, to determine whether a given element is a metal or a nonmetal, and to determine the group (chemical family) and the period of a given element.

11. Determine the valence shell number, the number of valence electrons, and the usual ionic charge of an atom from its position in the Periodic Chart.

12. State the Octet Rule and explain its use as a basis for describing compound formation.

13. Predict the type of bonding that two elements will undergo when they form a compound.

14. Describe covalent bonding and list general properties of covalent compounds.

15. Draw Lewis dot formulas for covalent compounds that include single, double, and triple bonds.

16. Identify polar and nonpolar covalent bonds using electronegativity values.

17. Describe ionic bonding and list general properties of ionic compounds.

18. Predict ionic compound formulas using ionic charges.

19. Write names from formulas and formulas from names for binary covalent, binary ionic, and ternary ionic compounds.

20. Calculate molecular masses for given covalent compounds and formula masses for given ionic compounds.

21. Explain the mole concept.

22. State the relationships that exist among moles, numbers of atoms, molecules, or formula units, and grams for a given substance.

23. Solve a variety of mole-Avogadro number problems using the conversion factor method.

UNIT IV: CHEMICAL REACTIONS

After completing this unit, students should be able to:

1. Interpret the symbols used in writing chemical equations.

2. Identify the reactants and products in a chemical reaction.

3. Balance chemical equations.

4. Write a balanced chemical equation given a verbal description of a chemical change.

5. Explain the terms exothermic reaction, endothermic reaction, and catalyst.

6. State the Law of Conservation of Mass and explain its significance with respect to chemical reactions.

7. State the relative numbers of atoms, molecules, and/or formula units represented in a balanced chemical equation.

8. State the relative numbers of moles of each chemical represented in a balanced chemical equation.

9. Determine the relative masses of each chemical represented in a balanced chemical equation.

10. Solve a variety of stoichiometry problems (mole-mole, mole-mass, mass-mass) using the conversion factor method.

11. Define actual yield, theoretical yield, and percent yield.

12. Classify chemical reactions as combination, decomposition, single displacement, double displacement, or combustion reactions.

UNIT V: SOLUTIONS

After completing this unit, students should be able to:

1. Define the terms solution, solute, and solvent and identify the solute and solvent in a given solution.

2. List the general properties of solutions.

3. Define the term solubility and explain how unsaturated, saturated, and supersaturated solutions are prepared.

4. Describe how the bonding nature of the solute and solvent, temperature, pressure, solute particle size, and agitation affect the dissolving process.

5. Explain the use of molarity and mass/mass percent as concentration units and perform a variety of concentration calculations.

6. Describe how solutions of a given molar concentration and a given mass/mass percent concentration are prepared in the laboratory.

7. Define the terms electrolyte and nonelectrolyte and explain the difference between a weak and a strong electrolyte.

8. Draw pictorial representations and write chemical equations for the dissolution of glucose, sodium chloride, acetic acid, and hydrogen chloride in water.

9. State differences between solutions and colloids.

UNIT VI: ACIDS AND BASES

After completing this unit, students should be able to:

1. Describe the auto-ionization of water and explain the formation of hydronium ions.

2. State the Arrhenius and the Brønsted-Lowry definitions of acids and bases.

3. Write chemical equations that show what occurs when Arrhenius acids and bases are added to water.

4. Label the Brønsted-Lowry acids and bases in a given chemical equation.

5. Give names and formulas for common acids (hydrochloric, sulfuric, nitric, phosphoric, carbonic, and acetic acid) and bases (sodium, potassium, magnesium, and calcium hydroxide and ammonia).

6. Describe the differences between strong and weak acids and between strong and weak bases.

7. Explain the process of acid-base neutralization and write balanced chemical equations for neutralization reactions.

8. Write balanced chemical equations for reactions between metals and acids and between acids and metal carbonates.

9. Define pH and explain the relationships between pH and hydrogen ion concentration and between hydrogen ion and hydroxide ion concentrations.

10. State where pH values for strong acids, weak acids, neutral solutions, weak bases, and strong bases are located on the pH scale.

11. Solve a variety of numerical problems involving the calculation of pH values, hydrogen ion concentrations, and hydroxide ion concentrations.

UNIT VII: INTRODUCTION TO ORGANIC CHEMISTRY

NOTE - This unit will be covered if time permits.

After completing this unit, students should be able to:

1. State differences between organic and inorganic compounds.

2. Describe the unique bonding characteristics of carbon atoms and explain why there are so many carbon compounds.

3. Identify hydrocarbons and list some of their general chemical and physical properties.

4. Write molecular formulas, structural formulas, and names for the first six straight-chain alkanes.

5. Classify organic compounds into different families (alcohols, carboxylic acids, amines) using the concept of functional groups.

6. Identify alcohols, carboxylic acids, and amines and list some of their general chemical and physical properties.

7. Define the term isomer and draw structural formulas for isomers of simple alkanes and alcohols.

8. Define the terms monomer, polymer, and polymerization.

9. Name several common polymers encountered in everyday life (polyethylene, teflon, polyvinyl chloride, etc.) and identify their monomer units.

LECTURE SUPPLEMENT

_____

REVIEW SHEETS

METRIC SYSTEM

Introduction

The metric system is a measurement system that was established in France in the 1790s. It consists of a set of base units that correspond to various physical quantities to be measured and a group of prefixes that are used with each base unit to form a series of units having different sizes. Each prefix corresponds to a power of 10. Therefore, each metric unit is related in size to other units of the same type by a power of 10, making the metric system a decimal system of measurement.

Use of the metric system gradually spread from France to many other countries and also to the scientific community. The modern version of the metric system is called the International System of Units, or SI. It is the official system of measurement used by most countries in the world and the system of choice of scientists.

Common metric units

The following table contains a list of several metric units that will be encountered frequently in the study of chemistry. Some metric-English equivalents are given to help you appreciate the sizes of metric units in comparison to other units. It is very important that you are familiar with the units in this list.

Physical quantity	Metric unit	Abbreviation	Metric-English equivalent
length	meter	m	1 m = 39.4 in 1 m = 1.09 yd
mass	gram	g	1 lb = 454 g 1 oz = 28.3 g
time	second	s	1 min = 60 s
volume	liter cubic meter	L m^3	1 L = 1.06 qt 1 gal = 3.79 L
heat	calorie joule	cal J	
temperature	degree Celsius kelvin	°C K	0 °C = 32 °F 100 °C = 212 °F

Metric prefixes

In the metric system, units of different sizes are obtained by using various prefixes in conjunction with the base metric units. For example, consider units for measuring length. The base unit is the meter (m). By using the prefix kilo- (k), which means 1000, we obtain the kilometer (km) as a length unit 1000 times larger than the base unit. The numerical values associated with the prefixes are always powers of 10 (1000 = 10^3). Any prefix can be used in conjunction with any base metric unit. The following table contains a list of metric prefixes that will be encountered frequently in the study of chemistry.

Metric prefix	Abbreviation	Numerical value
mega-	M	1,000,000 or 10^6
kilo-	k	1000 or 10^3
centi-	c	0.01 or 10^{-2}
milli-	m	0.001 or 10^{-3}
micro-	μ	0.000001 or 10^{-6}

The following examples illustrate use of the metric prefixes. In each example, a metric unit involving a prefix is related to the base unit and also to another unit involving a different prefix. Note that the units are always related in size by powers of 10.

Length - megameter   1 Mm = 1,000,000 m = 1000 km

Mass - kilogram   1 kg = 1000 g   = 1,000,000 mg

Length - centimeter   1 cm = 0.01 m   = 10 mm

Volume - milliliter   1 mL = 0.001 L   = 0.1 cL

Time - microsecond   1 μs = 0.000001 s   = 0.001 ms

It is often convenient to reverse some of these relationships. For example, 1 mL = 0.001 L can be expressed as 1 L = 1000 mL. These are equivalent expressions conveying the same information. As additional examples, it is easy to see that 1 cm = 0.01 m is equivalent to 1 m = 100 cm and that 1 μs = 0.000001 s can be expressed as 1 s = 1,000,000 μs.

Derived units

Once certain physical quantities and their units are defined, other physical quantities and their associated units can be derived from these defined quantities. As an example, consider units for measuring area. To determine the area of a rectangle, you would actually measure the length and the width of the rectangle and then compute the area by multiplying the length by the width. If the length and width are measured in meters (m), the area will have units of square meters (m x m = m^2). Thus, the area unit, square meter, is derived from the length unit, meter. The following table contains a list of some derived quantities and some units that can be used to measure these quantities.

Physical quantity	Defining equation	Possible derived units
area	area of a rectangle = length x width	m^2, km^2, cm^2
volume	volume of a rectangular solid = length x width x height	m^3, mm^3, cm^3
density	density = mass/volume	g/cm^3, kg/m^3, g/mL, g/L
speed	speed = distance/time	m/s, km/s, cm/s, cm/ms

Numerical relationships between derived units can be obtained, or derived, from other known relationships. For example, area and volume unit relationships can be derived from length unit relationships. The following examples illustrate this.

Length	Area	Volume
1 m = 100 cm	$(1\ m)^2 = (100\ cm)^2$ $1\ m^2 = 10000\ cm^2$ $1\ m^2 = 10^4\ cm^2$	$(1\ m)^3 = (100\ cm)^3$ $1\ m^3 = 1000000\ cm^3$ $1\ m^3 = 10^6\ cm^3$
1 in = 2.54 cm	$(1\ in)^2 = (2.54\ cm)^2$ $1\ in^2 = 6.45\ cm^2$	$(1\ in)^3 = (2.54\ cm)^3$ $1\ in^3 = 16.4\ cm^3$

It is very helpful to understand the concept of derived units. You do not need to memorize or look up every possible numerical relationship between units. If you know some key relationships, you can usually derive many other relationships. As seen in the examples above, a knowledge of length units allows you to obtain area and volume relationships. Learn lengths and derive areas and volumes when you need them.

Additional information and relationships

The following table contains some useful information regarding several metric units. Numerical relationships between different units are listed. These can help you to appreciate the size of a particular unit in comparison to other units, and they can be used as conversion factors in unit conversion problems.

Physical quantity	Information and conversion factors
length	1 m = 39.4 in = 3.28 ft = 1.09 yd 1 in = 2.54 cm (exact) 1 km = 0.621 mile A U.S. dime is about 1 mm, or 0.1 cm, thick. Atoms have diameters of about 10^{-8} cm.
mass	1 lb = 454 g 1 oz = 28.3 g 1 kg = 2.20 lb A U.S. nickel has a mass of about 5 g. Atoms have masses in the range 10^{-24} to 10^{-22} g.
volume	1 L = 1000 mL = 1.06 qt 1 gal = 3.79 L 1 mL = 1 cm^3 1 m^3 = 1000 L 1 in^3 = 16.4 cm^3
density	1 g/mL = 1 g/cm^3 = 1000 g/L = 1 kg/L = 1000 kg/m^3 1 g/mL = 2.09 lb/qt = 8.35 lb/gal = 62.4 lb/ft^3 Density of water at 4 °C = 1.00 g/mL
temperature	The degree sign (°) is not used for Kelvin temperatures. A 1 °C temperature change equals a 1.8 °F change. A 1 °C temperature change equals a 1 K change. Freezing point of water = 32 °F = 0 °C = 273 K Boiling point of water = 212 °F = 100 °C = 373 K Absolute zero = 0 K = -273 °C = -460 °F
heat	A calorie is the amount of heat needed to change the temperature of 1 g of liquid water by 1 °C. 1 cal = 4.18 J

CLASSIFICATION OF MATTER

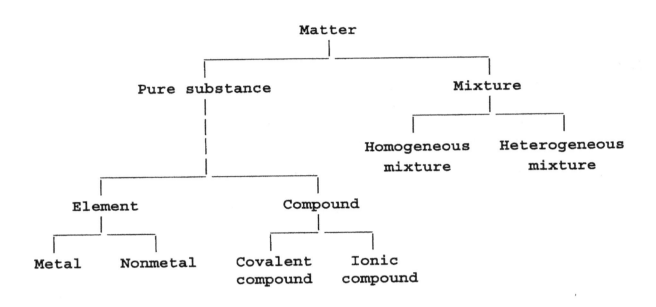

Matter – anything that has mass and occupies space

Mixture – two or more component substances
- variable composition
- component substances retain their chemical identity
- separate component substances by physical means
- homogeneous or heterogeneous

Pure substance – type of matter that cannot be separated into two or more components by physical means
- fixed, definite composition
- homogeneous

Element – pure substance that cannot be broken down into simpler substances by chemical means
- 114 elements listed on Periodic Chart
- natural vs. synthetic elements
- smallest unit is an atom (except diatomic elements)

Metal – shiny, metallic luster
- good electrical conductor
- good heat conductor
- solid at room temperature (except mercury)
- malleable and ductile
- atom forms cation (positive charge)
- located to left of stair-step line on Periodic Chart

Nonmetal – usually not an electrical conductor
- solid or gas at room temperature (except bromine)
- brittle solid state
- atom forms anion (negative charge)
- located to right of stair-step line on Periodic Chart

Compound – pure substance composed of two or more elements chemically combined in a fixed proportion by mass
- component elements lose their chemical identity
- separate component elements by chemical means
- millions of compounds

Covalent compound – contains two or more nonmetal elements
- solid, liquid, or gas at room temperature
- relatively low melting point (typically below 350 °C)
- typically does not conduct electricity when melted or dissolved in water
- smallest unit is a molecule

Ionic compound – contains metal and nonmetal elements
- solid at room temperature
- relatively high melting point (typically above 350 °C)
- conducts electricity when melted or dissolved in water
- smallest unit is a formula unit composed of cations and anions (not a molecule)

CLASSIFICATION EXAMPLES

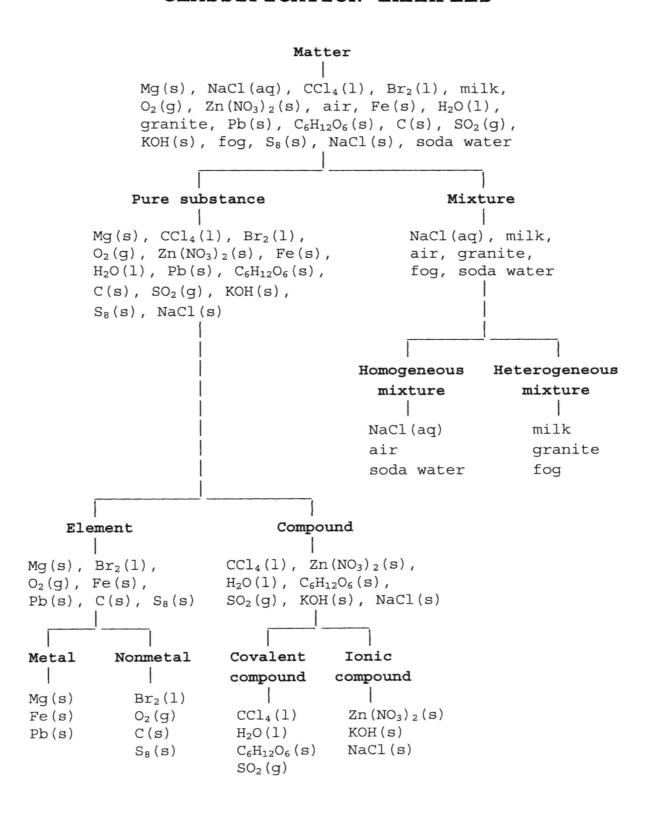

ELEMENTS

The following is a list of the elements that will be encountered frequently in the study of chemistry. It is important that you know the names, symbols, and common ions of these elements.

Element	Symbol	Common ion(s)	Element	Symbol	Common ion(s)
hydrogen	H	H^{1+}, H^{1-}	calcium	Ca	Ca^{2+}
helium	He		chromium	Cr	Cr^{3+}
lithium	Li	Li^{1+}	iron	Fe	Fe^{2+}, Fe^{3+}
beryllium	Be		cobalt	Co	Co^{2+}
boron	B		nickel	Ni	Ni^{2+}
carbon	C		copper	Cu	Cu^{1+}, Cu^{2+}
nitrogen	N	N^{3-}	zinc	Zn	Zn^{2+}
oxygen	O	O^{2-}	arsenic	As	
fluorine	F	F^{1-}	bromine	Br	Br^{1-}
neon	Ne		silver	Ag	Ag^{1+}
sodium	Na	Na^{1+}	tin	Sn	Sn^{2+}
magnesium	Mg	Mg^{2+}	iodine	I	I^{1-}
aluminum	Al	Al^{3+}	barium	Ba	Ba^{2+}
silicon	Si		platinum	Pt	
phosphorus	P	P^{3-}	gold	Au	
sulfur	S	S^{2-}	mercury	Hg	Hg_2^{2+}, Hg^{2+}
chlorine	Cl	Cl^{1-}	lead	Pb	Pb^{2+}
argon	Ar		radon	Rn	
potassium	K	K^{1+}	uranium	U	

Your instructor may add additional elements to this list. Enter them in the following table.

Element	Symbol	Common ion(s)	Element	Symbol	Common ion(s)

POLYATOMIC IONS

The following is a list of the polyatomic ions that will be encountered frequently in the study of chemistry. It is important that you know the names, formulas, and charges of these ions.

Polyatomic ion name	Formula with charge
phosphate ion	PO_4^{3-}
carbonate ion	CO_3^{2-}
sulfate ion	SO_4^{2-}
sulfite ion	SO_3^{2-}
cyanide ion	CN^{1-}
hydrogen carbonate ion*	HCO_3^{1-}
hydrogen sulfate ion	HSO_4^{1-}
hydrogen sulfite ion	HSO_3^{1-}
hydroxide ion	OH^{1-}
nitrate ion	NO_3^{1-}
nitrite ion	NO_2^{1-}
ammonium ion	NH_4^{1+}

* Commonly called bicarbonate ion.

Your instructor may add additional polyatomic ions to this list. Enter them in the following table.

Polyatomic ion name	Formula with charge

ELECTRONIC STRUCTURE OF ATOMS

Orbitals/quantized energy levels

The electrons in an atom are considered to occupy atomic orbitals. An orbital is a region in space around the nucleus where electrons have a high probability of being found. There are different types of orbitals, with each type having a characteristic electron density distribution, or shape, and a characteristic energy.

The energies of the orbitals are quantized. This means that each orbital in an atom has a fixed, definite energy value that is characteristic of that particular atom. When an electron occupies a certain orbital, it has the energy corresponding to that orbital. Therefore, the orbitals in an atom can also be considered as a set of quantized energy levels that electrons can occupy.

Electron energy level diagram for atoms

The quantized energy levels, or orbitals, of an atom can be displayed on an energy diagram in order to show their relative energies. In the following diagram, the energy levels are represented by dashes (-).

↑ E N E R G Y ↑	1st shell	2nd shell	3rd shell	4th shell	7s _ 6p _ _ _ 5d _ _ _ _ _
				4f _ _ _ _ _ _ _	6s _ 5p _ _ _
				4d _ _ _ _ _	5s _
				4p _ _ _	
			3d _ _ _ _ _	4s _	5th, 6th, 7th shells (incomplete)
			3p _ _ _ 3s _		
		2p _ _ _ 2s _			
	1s _				

The energy levels can be divided into certain sets based on their energies. Each of these sets of energy levels is called an electron shell, which is identified by an integer number. In general, electrons in higher shells have greater energies and are more likely found farther from the nucleus than electrons in lower shells.

The energy levels, or orbitals, in each shell can be divided into subshells, which are identified by the letters s, p, d, and f. An s subshell contains just one orbital. A p subshell contains three orbitals that are of equal energy. The d and f subshells contain five and seven orbitals, respectively. The number of subshells in a given shell equals the shell number. For example, the 3rd shell contains 3 subshells – s, p, and d. By using the shell number and subshell letter, each subshell can be given a unique label (1s, 2s, 2p, etc.).

Maximum electron capacities

Each orbital, subshell, and shell of an atom has a maximum number of electrons that it can hold. An individual orbital can hold a maximum of two electrons. Using this fact, the maximum electron capacities of the subshells and shells can easily be calculated. This information is given in the following tables.

Subshell	Number of orbitals	Max. number of electrons
s	1	2
p	3	6
d	5	10
f	7	14

Shell	Subshells present	Max. number of electrons
1	s	2
2	s p	8
3	s p d	18
4	s p d f	32

Order of filling atomic orbitals/energy levels

An atom is normally found in its ground electronic state, which is the lowest energy electronic state of that atom. In order to obtain this lowest energy state, the orbitals of an atom must be filled with electrons in a specific way. We start with the orbital having the lowest energy and place electrons into the orbitals in the order of their increasing energies. An orbital must be completely filled with electrons before we can start filling the next orbital of higher energy. The order in which the orbitals must be filled for the ground electronic state of an atom is obtained by following the arrows in the diagram below. Compare this order with the energy level diagram given above.

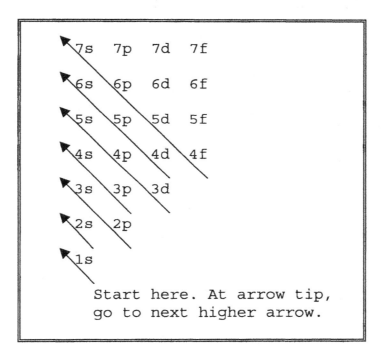

Electron configurations

The electron configuration of an atom is a statement of how the electrons of the atom are distributed in the various orbitals, or energy levels. We are interested in the ground state electron configuration since an atom is normally found in its lowest energy state. To obtain this electron configurations, we must place the electrons into the orbitals in the order describe above. Also, we must not exceed the maximum electron capacities given above for the orbitals, subshells, and shells.

Ground state electron configurations for several atoms are given below. Each subshell is indicated by its shell number and subshell letter label. The number of electrons in each subshell is indicated by a number written as a superscript.

H	$1s^1$	Na	$1s^2 2s^2 2p^6 3s^1$
He	$1s^2$	P	$1s^2 2s^2 2p^6 3s^2 3p^3$
		Ar	$1s^2 2s^2 2p^6 3s^2 3p^6$
Li	$1s^2 2s^1$		
Be	$1s^2 2s^2$	K	$1s^2 2s^2 2p^6 3s^2 3p^6 4s^1$
B	$1s^2 2s^2 2p^1$	Fe	$1s^2 2s^2 2p^6 3s^2 3p^6 4s^2 3d^6$
N	$1s^2 2s^2 2p^3$	As	$1s^2 2s^2 2p^6 3s^2 3p^6 4s^2 3d^{10} 4p^3$
Ne	$1s^2 2s^2 2p^6$	Kr	$1s^2 2s^2 2p^6 3s^2 3p^6 4s^2 3d^{10} 4p^6$

Valence shell/valence electrons

The valence shell of an atom is the highest energy shell of that atom. Electrons in this shell are called valence electrons. The valence electrons are more likely found farther from the nucleus than the other electrons in an atom. For this reason, the valence shell is also called the outer shell of an atom. We can obtain information about an atom's valence shell and valence electrons from its electron configuration. Consider the valence information for nitrogen, phosphorus, and arsenic listed in the following table.

Atom	Electron configuration	Valence shell number	Number of valence electrons	Valence shell configuration
N	$1s^2 2s^2 2p^3$	2nd	5	$2s^2 2p^3$
P	$1s^2 2s^2 2p^6 3s^2 3p^3$	3rd	5	$3s^2 3p^3$
As	$1s^2 2s^2 2p^6 3s^2 3p^6 4s^2 3d^{10} 4p^3$	4th	5	$4s^2 4p^3$

Why is it important to know about valence electrons? The answer is that the chemical properties of an element are determined by the number and arrangement of its valence electrons. For example, the chemical properties of nitrogen can be explained by the fact that nitrogen atoms have five valence electrons arranged in the configuration $2s^2 2p^3$.

The vertical columns of elements on the Periodic Table are called chemical families or groups. Elements in the same family have similar chemical properties. The reason for this is that chemical properties are determined by valence electrons, and elements in the same family have the same number and arrangement of valence electrons. Nitrogen, phosphorus, and arsenic are members of the nitrogen family of elements, and, as such, they have some chemical similarities. The table above shows that nitrogen, phosphorus, and arsenic atoms each have five valence electrons arranged in the configuration ns^2np^3.

COMPOUNDS AND CHEMICAL BONDING

Octet Rule

Elements combine with each other to form compounds. For example, carbon and oxygen combine to form carbon dioxide. In terms of the smallest units that make up substances, atoms of elements bond together to form molecules and formula units of compounds. For example, one carbon atom and two oxygen atoms bond together to form a carbon dioxide molecule.

The basis for understanding chemical bonding in many compounds is the Octet Rule. This rule states that atoms have a tendency to acquire eight valence electrons. This gives them the stable valence shell electron configuration of noble gas atoms.

Atoms can acquire eight valence electrons by sharing pairs of electrons with other atoms or by gaining or losing electrons to form ions. These two different mechanisms that allow atoms to satisfy the Octet Rule lead to two different types of chemical bonding and two general types of compounds. These are covalent and ionic bonding, and covalent and ionic compounds. Covalent compounds are also referred to as molecular compounds.

Atoms that already have eight valence electrons are quite stable and, therefore, do not have a tendency to form chemical bonds. This is the case for the noble gases. With a few exceptions, these elements do not form compounds.

Finally, there are two important exceptions to the Octet Rule. These are hydrogen and helium atoms, which require only two valence electrons.

Covalent bonding/covalent (or molecular) compounds

1. Nonmetal elements combine with each other to form covalent compounds. Some examples are CO_2, H_2O, NI_3, C_2H_6, SO_3, CCl_4, $C_6H_{12}O_6$, and H_2SO_4.

2. When a covalent compound forms from its elements, atoms of the elements share pairs of electrons in order to obtain eight valence electrons and satisfy the Octet Rule. Two nonmetal atoms can share one, two, or three pairs of electrons, and the shared electrons belong to both atoms.

3. In a covalent compound, certain atoms are close enough together to form units in which the atoms share pairs of electrons. Electrical forces of attraction between the shared electrons and each of the two atoms that are sharing them hold the atoms together as a unit. The force of attraction between the atoms and the shared electrons is called a covalent bond. Covalent bonds can be single, double, or triple bonds depending on the number of pairs of electrons that are shared.

4. The smallest unit of a covalent compound is called a molecule. Carbon dioxide is composed of CO_2 molecules, each of which consists of one C atom and two O atoms linked together by covalent bonds.

5. A covalent compound is represented by a molecular formula, which gives the exact number of each kind of atom present in a molecule of the substance, and by a Lewis dot formula, which indicates the chemical bonding in a molecule. For carbon dioxide, the molecular formula CO_2 and the dot formula :Ö::C::Ö: show that the molecules are composed of one C atom and two O atoms linked together by double covalent bonds.

6. Covalent compounds have certain general properties.

   A. Covalent compounds have relatively low melting points (typically below 350 °C). For example, $H_2O(s)$ (ice) melts at 0 °C.

   B. Covalent compounds are solids, liquids, or gases at room temperature (25 °C), depending on the melting and boiling points of the particular compound. There is not a common physical state for these compounds at room temperature. For example, at 25 °C, CO_2 is a gas, H_2O is a liquid, and $C_6H_{12}O_6$ is a solid.

   C. Many covalent compounds, especially organic compounds, are insoluble in water.

   D. Covalent compounds typically do not conduct electricity when melted or when dissolved in water. This results from the fact that these compounds are composed of neutral molecular units. Acids, which conduct electricity because they ionize when dissolved in water, are an exception.

Ionic bonding/ionic compounds

1. Metal elements combine with nonmetal elements to form ionic compounds. Some examples are NaCl, K_2S, MgO, $CaBr_2$, ZnS, $CuCl_2$, Mg_3N_2, and NaH.

2. When an ionic compound forms from its elements, atoms of the metal element lose their valence electrons to form positive ions (cations), which have eight electrons in their valence shells and satisfy the Octet Rule. The electrons lost by the metal atoms are gained by the atoms of the nonmetal element to form negative ions (anions), which also obey the Octet Rule.

3. In an ionic compound in the solid state, the cations and anions are packed very close together in a neat, orderly array with cations surrounded by anions and anions surrounded by cations. Electrical forces of attraction between oppositely charged ions hold all the ions together in the solid crystal. The force of attraction between oppositely charged ions is called an ionic bond.

4. The smallest unit of an ionic compound is called a formula unit. Potassium sulfide is composed of K_2S formula units, each of which consists of two K^{1+} ions and one S^{2-} ion linked together by ionic bonds. Since an ionic compound consists of an array of cations and anions, a certain combination of these ions can be selected as a smallest unit of the compound. However, this is not the same as a molecule because these ions are not bonded exclusively to one another as the atoms in a molecule are. A cation in an ionic crystal attracts every anion around it, and vice versa.

5. An ionic compound is represented by an empirical formula, which gives the smallest whole number ratio of the numbers of the different ions present in a sample of the substance. For potassium sulfide, the empirical formula K_2S shows that there are two times as many K^{1+} ions as there are S^{2-} ions in a sample of the compound. This two-to-one ratio of the ions is necessary for the compound to be electrically neutral.

6. Ionic compounds have certain general properties.

   A. Ionic compounds have relatively high melting points (typically above 350 °C). For example, NaCl(s) (table salt) melts at 801 °C.

B. Ionic compounds are solids at room temperature (25 °C).

C. Many ionic compounds are soluble in water.

D. Ionic compounds conduct electricity when melted or when dissolved in water. This results from the fact that these compounds are composed of positive and negative ions that can readily move when the substance is melted or dissolved.

SOLUTIONS

Basic definitions

1. Solution – homogeneous, non-separating (on standing) mixture
        of two or more substances

2. Solute – substance that is dissolved, usually present in the
        smaller amount, usually the active component of a
        solution in chemical reactions

3. Solvent – substance that does the dissolving, usually present
        in the larger amount, usually the inactive
        component of a solution in chemical reactions

Consider an aqueous solution of sodium chloride, $NaCl(aq)$.
$NaCl(s)$ is the solute, and $H_2O(l)$ is the solvent.

In the reaction $NaCl(aq) + AgNO_3(aq) \rightarrow NaNO_3(aq) + AgCl(s)$, the
NaCl takes an active part in the chemical change, while the H_2O
is inactive and does not react.

Types of solutions

Solutions can be classified according to the physical states of
the solute and the solvent. Some examples are given in the
following table.

Solvent → Solute ↓	Gas	Liquid	Solid
Gas	air (mainly $O_2(g)$ in $N_2(g)$)	soda water ($CO_2(g)$ in $H_2O(l)$)	$H_2(g)$ in $Pd(s)$
Liquid	Do not exist.	ethyl alcohol(l) in $H_2O(l)$	$Hg(l)$ in $Ag(s)$ (an amalgam)
Solid	Do not exist.	$NaCl(aq)$ ($NaCl(s)$ in $H_2O(l)$)	brass ($Zn(s)$ in $Cu(s)$)

Note that a solution exists in one physical state. For example,
when solid NaCl is dissolved in liquid H_2O, the resulting
solution is liquid.

While several types of solutions are listed in this table, the
solutions most frequently encountered in basis chemistry are
those that have a liquid solvent.

Properties of solutions

1. Retention of chemical identity of components

   The physical process of making a solution does not change the chemical identity of either the solute or the solvent.

2. Variable composition

   Aqueous solutions of sodium chloride do not all have the same composition. For example, 5 g of NaCl or 10 g of NaCl can be dissolved in 100 mL of H_2O to form solutions of two different compositions.

   In contrast, chemical compounds have fixed compositions. Every sample of a particular compound contains the same component elements combined in the same definite proportion by mass (Law of Definite Proportions).

3. Separation of components by physical means

   The components of an aqueous solution of sodium chloride can be separated by boiling the solution. At the boiling temperature, sodium chloride is not volatile and will remain behind as the water is converted into steam. The steam can be condensed back into liquid water. Boiling and condensation are physical processes.

4. Homogeneity

   Solutions are always uniform throughout in terms of their composition and properties.

5. Non-separation of components on standing

   For example, compare what happens when sodium chloride, sand, and water are mixed together and stirred. The sodium chloride quickly dissolves in the water. The sand, however, is merely dispersed in the water; it does not dissolve. When stirring is stopped and the mixture is allowed to stand undisturbed, the sodium chloride will stay mixed with the water, while the sand will begin to separate and settle out of the water.

6. Transparency (liquid and gas solutions)

   An aqueous solution of copper(II) nitrate is blue in color, but it is perfectly clear.

Factors that affect the dissolving process

1. Bonding nature of solute and solvent – "like dissolves like"

   Polar and ionic solutes tend to dissolve in polar solvents. Nonpolar solutes tend to dissolve in nonpolar solvents. Polar and nonpolar substances tend not to dissolve in one another.

   Consider the following common substances.

Substance	Bonding nature
water	polar covalent
ethyl alcohol	polar covalent
motor oil	nonpolar covalent
dry cleaning fluid	nonpolar covalent
table salt	ionic

   Ethyl alcohol and table salt dissolve in water. Motor oil dissolves in dry cleaning fluid. Motor oil and water do not mix together to form a solution.

2. Temperature – effect on both rate of dissolving and amount of solute that dissolves

   Rate: Solids tend to dissolve faster in liquids when the temperature is increased.

   Compare the rates at which sugar dissolves in iced tea and in hot tea.

   Amount: For most solids, the maximum amount of the solid that will dissolve in a given amount of a liquid increases when the temperature is increased.

   Compare the maximum amounts of sugar that can be dissolved in equal quantities of hot tea and iced tea.

   Amount: For most gases, the maximum amount of the gas that will dissolve in a given amount of a liquid decreases when the temperature increases.

   Consider what happens when a pan of tap water is warmed on a stove. The water contains dissolved air that tends to come out of solution and form tiny gas bubbles on the sides of the pan as the temperature increases.

3. Pressure - effect on solubility of gases

   Henry's Law: The amount of a gas that dissolves in a given
              amount of a liquid is directly proportional to
              the partial pressure of the gas above the
              liquid.

   Consider the noise that you hear and the bubbles that you see
   when you open a bottle of a carbonated beverage. The noise is
   produced by carbon dioxide gas rapidly escaping from the
   space above the liquid when the bottle is opened. The bubbles
   are produced be dissolved carbon dioxide coming out of the
   liquid in response to the decrease in carbon dioxide pressure
   above the liquid.

4. Solute particle size - effect on rate of dissolving

   Grinding a solid into smaller particles generally increases
   the rate at which it dissolves in a liquid. The grinding
   process increases the surface area of the solid. Increasing
   the surface area over which a liquid can come into contact
   with the solid will increase the rate at which the solid
   dissolves. However, grinding a solid into smaller particles
   will not change the maximum amount of the solid that can be
   dissolved in a given amount of a liquid.

5. Agitation - effect on rate of dissolving

   Stirring or shaking generally increases the rate at which a
   solid dissolves in a liquid. Sugar will dissolve in iced tea
   without stirring, but the process is rather slow. Stirring
   will speed up the dissolution of the sugar. However, stirring
   will not change the maximum amount of sugar that can be
   dissolved in a given amount of the tea.

Additional terms

1. Solubility - maximum amount of solute that will dissolve in a
              given amount of a solvent at a given temperature

   Consider the solubility of potassium nitrate in water as an
   example. At 25 °C, a maximum of 38 g KNO_3 can be dissolved in
   100 g H_2O. At 75 °C, a maximum of 155 g KNO_3 can be dissolved
   in 100 g H_2O. A common unit for reporting solubility values is
   grams of solute per 100 grams of solvent.

2. Saturated solution – solution that contains the maximum amount of solute that will dissolve in a given amount of a solvent at a given temperature

The terms "solubility" and "saturated solution" are related. To measure the solubility of a substance, you must prepare a saturated solution of that substance.

In addition to being saturated, solutions can be unsaturated or supersaturated. An unsaturated solution contains less than the maximum amount of solute that the solvent can dissolve; a supersaturated solution contains more than the maximum amount of solute. Supersaturated solutions are usually prepared by making a saturated solution at a certain temperature and then cooling the solution to a lower temperature. If precipitation does not occur, the cooled solution will be supersaturated.

3. Dilution – process of preparing a less concentrated solution from a more concentrated solution by addition of solvent

For example, consider that your morning coffee is too strong for your taste. You add water to the coffee to dilute it and make it more palatable.

4. Miscible liquids – liquids that mix together to form a solution

Immiscible liquids – liquids that do not mix together to form a solution

Water and ethyl alcohol are miscible liquids. Water and motor oil are immiscible.

5. Electrolyte – substance that conducts electricity when dissolved in water

Nonelectrolyte – substance that does not conduct electricity when dissolved in water

Table salt (NaCl, sodium chloride) is an electrolyte, while table sugar ($C_{12}H_{22}O_{11}$, sucrose) is a nonelectrolyte.

LECTURE SUPPLEMENT

_____

WORKSHEETS

SIGNIFICANT FIGURES AND SCIENTIFIC NOTATION

1. Indicate the number of significant figures in each of the following numbers and convert them to or from scientific notation.

   a. 43.55

   b. 5.67×10^2

   c. 0.00346

   d. 3×10^{-6}

   e. 2.7×10^3

   f. 1201.0

   g. 1201

   h. 13004.1

   i. 1.4040×10^6

   j. 8.0×10^{-2}

2. Round off each of the following numbers to four significant figures and convert the rounded values to or from scientific notation.

   a. 4,567,985

   b. 2.3581×10^3

   c. 0.00463537

   d. 90.4483

   e. 9.0373×10^{-5}

   f. 0.0000083839

   g. 1.938876×10^3

   h. 200.032

3. Perform the following calculations and express each answer to the correct number of significant figures.

   a. 3.22×0.17

   b. $4568/1.3$

   c. $22.8 - 0.032$

   d. $0.0003/16$

   e. $(12.3 + 0.092)/8.3$

   f. $328 \times (0.125 + 5.43)$

   g. $21.53 + 0.143 + 3.8$

   h. $1.987/(3.46 \times 10^8)$

4. Perform the following calculations using scientific notation.

   a. $(8.4 \times 10^3) \times (1.6 \times 10^{-5})$

   b. $(4.3 \times 10^3) + (6.8 \times 10^4)$

   c. $(3.2 \times 10^4)/(8.0 \times 10^{-7})$

   d. $(7.3 \times 10^{-5}) - (4.6 \times 10^{-6})$

   e. $(2.8 \times 10^2) \times (4.7 \times 10^{-4})/(1.6 \times 10^{-5})$

UNIT CONVERSIONS

1. Perform the following metric-metric unit conversions.

   a. 2.85×10^4 cm to m

   b. 7.32×10^2 g to kg

   c. 4.88×10^{-1} L to mL

   d. 3.65×10^{-2} kcal to cal

   e. 1.92 kg to mg

   f. 258 mm to cm

   g. 0.0657 ms to μs

   h. 2750 cm to Mm

2. Perform the following metric-English unit conversions.

   a. 25.3 lb to g

   b. 785 cm to in

   c. 92700 ms to min

   d. 4.31 qt to mL

   e. 0.275 km to mile

   f. 3.95 oz to μg

3. Perform the following area and volume conversions.

   a. 0.0263 km^2 to m^2

   b. 4.35 m^3 to L

   c. 585 cm^2 to in^2

   d. 1.25 ft^3 to m^3

   e. 75.2 mL to cm^3

   f. 0.317 gal to mL

4. Perform the following density conversions.

   a. 1.00 g/mL to g/cm^3

   b. 2.75 g/cm^3 to kg/m^3

   c. 4.21 kg/m^3 to g/L

   d. 9.35 lb/gal to g/mL

5. Perform the following temperature conversions.

   a. 98.6 °F to °C

   b. 0 K to °F

   c. 212 °F to K

   d. -40 °C to °F

ATOMIC STRUCTURE

1. Characterize the three subatomic particles that make up atoms by completing the following table. (1 amu = 1.67×10^{-24} g)

Particle	Charge	Mass (amu)	Location in atom
proton			
neutron			
electron			

2. Draw a sketch illustrating the Rutherford (nuclear) model of the atom. Indicate how the protons, electrons, and neutrons are arranged in the atom. Give approximate values for the diameter of the nucleus, the diameter of the atom, and the mass of the atom.

3. Complete the following table using the given information and a Periodic Chart.

Element symbol	Atomic number	Mass number	# of protons	# of electrons	# of neutrons
Ca		41			
	15				16
		65	30		
U					143
	17	37			
				56	81

4. Define the term isotope. Characterize the three isotopes of hydrogen by completing the following table.

Isotope	# of protons	# of electrons	# of neutrons	Mass (amu)
$_{1}^{1}H$				
$_{1}^{2}H$				
$_{1}^{3}H$				

ELECTRONIC STRUCTURE OF ATOMS

1. Write a complete electron configuration for each of the following atoms.

   a. H   c. F   e. S   g. Fe

   b. C   d. Mg   f. K   h. Kr

2. Give the valence shell number and the number of valence electrons for each of the following atoms. Also, draw a Lewis electron dot formula for each.

Atom	Valence shell number	# of valence electrons	Electron dot formula
F			
Mg			
S			
K			
Kr			

3. Indicate whether the following atoms gain or lose electrons to form stable ions. Give the number of electrons that each gains or loses and write a symbol for each ion.

Atom	Gain or lose electrons	# of electrons	Symbol for ion
F			
Mg			
S			
K			
Kr			

BONDING AND CHEMICAL FORMULAS

1. State the Octet Rule. Explain two ways in which a sulfur atom can obey the Octet Rule.

2. Predict whether the following substances have ionic, nonpolar covalent, or polar covalent bonds.

   a. H_2O c. S_8 e. SO_2

   b. $MgCl_2$ d. LiF   f. H_2

3. Draw Lewis electron dot formulas for the following molecules.

   a. H_2O c. CO_2 e. SO_2

   b. N_2 d. CCl_4 f. HBr

4. Write formulas for compounds containing the following elements.

   a. potassium and chlorine   d. sodium and nitrogen

   b. magnesium and iodine   e. aluminum and sulfur

   c. calcium and oxygen   f. lithium and oxygen

5. Explain how both ionic and covalent bonding are involved in the compound $Ca(NO_3)_2$.

190

NOMENCLATURE

1. a. By examining its formula, how can you determine whether a chemical compound is a covalent or an ionic compound?

   b. Why is it necessary to determine this before naming the compound?

2. Name the following binary covalent compounds.

   a. NO c. N_2O e. PBr_3 g. SF_6
   b. NO_2 d. N_2O_5 f. CS_2 h. N_2Cl_4

3. Name the following ionic compounds.

   a. Mg_3N_2 d. $CuCl_2$ g. Ag_3PO_4 j. $Ca(HCO_3)_2$
   b. $Mg(NO_2)_2$ e. KBr h. Na_2O k. $(NH_4)_2S$
   c. $Mg(NO_3)_2$ f. $Ba(OH)_2$ i. $Fe_2(SO_4)_3$ l. Cu_2CO_3

4. Write formulas for the following binary covalent compounds.

   a. carbon tetraiodide   e. iodine monobromide
   b. dichlorine trioxide   f. boron trifluoride
   c. arsenic trichloride   g. oxygen difluoride
   d. sulfur dioxide   h. diphosphorus pentoxide

5. Write formulas for the following ionic compounds.

   a. sodium sulfide   g. iron(III) chloride
   b. sodium sulfite   h. zinc sulfide
   c. sodium sulfate   i. copper(II) phosphate
   d. sodium hydrogen sulfate   j. aluminum hydroxide
   e. nickel(II) carbonate   k. lead(II) nitrate
   f. potassium cyanide   l. sodium bicarbonate

MOLE CALCULATIONS

1. Fill in the blanks. O_2 is oxygen gas or elemental oxygen, which exists as a diatomic molecule. O is atomic oxygen, and O_3 is ozone.

   1 mole O_2 = _____ O_2 molecules = _____ g O_2

   1 mole O = _____ O atoms   = _____ g O

   1 mole O_3 = _____ O_3 molecules = _____ g O_3

2. Calculate the molar mass of each of the following compounds.

   a. NaCl   c. H_2SO_4 e. $C_6H_{12}O_6$

   b. CO_2 d. $Ca(NO_3)_2$ f. $Fe_2(SO_4)_3$

3. Calculate the number of moles and the number of molecules contained in each of the following samples.

   a. 55 g CO_2 c. 1.2 kg H_2SO_4

   b. 0.25 g H_2SO_4 d. 15 mg $C_6H_{12}O_6$

4. Calculate the mass in grams of each of the following samples.

   a. 0.75 mole $Ca(NO_3)_2$ c. 1.0×10^{25} O_2 molecules

   b. 1.5 moles NaCl   d. 2.5×10^{20} CO_2 molecules

5. Calculate the number of oxygen atoms in each of the following samples.

   a. 8.7×10^{21} O_3 molecules

   b. 15 moles H_2SO_4

   c. 100 g CO_2

BALANCING CHEMICAL EQUATIONS

1. Consider the following balanced chemical equation.

$$3 \ Ca(NO_3)_2 \ + \ 2 \ Na_3PO_4 \ \rightarrow \ 6 \ NaNO_3 \ + \ Ca_3(PO_4)_2$$

   a. Identify the reactants and the products in the equation.

   b. What are the numbers in front of each of the chemical formulas called?

   c. How many calcium nitrate formula units are represented on the left side of the equation?

   d. How many calcium phosphate formula units are represented on the right side?

   e. How many oxygen atoms are represented on each side of the equation?

2. Balance the following chemical equations.

   a. __ CH_4 + __ O_2 → __ CO_2 + __ H_2O

   b. __ H_2 + __ O_2 → __ H_2O

   c. __ $CaCl_2$ + __ $AgNO_3$ → __ $Ca(NO_3)_2$ + __ $AgCl$

   d. __ N_2 + __ H_2 → __ NH_3

   e. __ $KClO_3$ → __ KCl + __ O_2

   f. __ Al + __ H_2SO_4 → __ $Al_2(SO_4)_3$ + __ H_2

   g. __ HNO_3 + __ $Mg(OH)_2$ → __ $Mg(NO_3)_2$ + __ H_2O

   h. __ C_2H_6O + __ O_2 → __ CO_2 + __ H_2O

   i. __ Na + __ H_2O → __ $NaOH$ + __ H_2

   j. __ Al + __ O_2 → __ Al_2O_3

STOICHIOMETRY CALCULATIONS

1. State the relative numbers of moles of the chemicals represented in the following balanced chemical equation. From these values, calculate the relative masses of the chemicals involved in the reaction.

$$H_2SO_4 \; + \; 2 \; NaOH \; \rightarrow \; Na_2SO_4 \; + \; 2 \; H_2O$$

2. State the Law of Conservation of Mass. Show how the relative masses determined in problem 1 can be used to illustrate this law.

3. Perform calculations a-e below using the following balanced chemical equation.

$$C_6H_{12}O_6 \, (aq) \; \rightarrow \; 2 \; CO_2 \, (g) \; + \; 2 \; C_2H_6O \, (aq)$$

   a. How many moles of $C_6H_{12}O_6$ are needed to produce 15.7 moles of C_2H_6O?

   b. How many grams of CO_2 are formed by the reaction of 2.58×10^2 moles of $C_6H_{12}O_6$?

   c. How many grams of C_2H_6O are formed by the reaction of 25.3 grams of $C_6H_{12}O_6$?

   d. How many grams of $C_6H_{12}O_6$ are needed to produce 8.57 millimoles of CO_2?

   e. How many grams of CO_2 are formed when 2.35 pounds of C_2H_6O are produced?

ACIDS AND BASES

1. a. State the Arrhenius definitions of an acid and a base.

   b. Write chemical equations that show HCl is an Arrhenius acid and NaOH is an Arrhenius base.

2. a. State the Brønsted-Lowry definitions of an acid and a base.

   b. Identify the Brønsted-Lowry acids and bases in the following chemical equations.

$$H_2S \; + \; H_2O \; \rightleftarrows \; H_3O^{1+} \; + \; HS^{1-}$$

$$NH_3 \; + \; H_2O \; \rightleftarrows \; NH_4^{1+} \; + \; OH^{1-}$$

3. Write chemical equations that show the ionization in aqueous solution of the strong acid HCl and the weak acid HCN. Explain the difference between these equations.

4. Write a balanced chemical equation for each of the following reactions.

   a. __ HCl(aq) + __ NaOH(aq) →

   b. __ Mg(s) + __ HCl(aq) →

   c. __ HCl(aq) + __ Na$_2$CO$_3$(aq) →

5. Indicate whether the following solutions are acidic, basic, or neutral. A solution with:

   a. pH = 10

   b. $[H^{1+}] = 1 \times 10^{-7}$ M

   c. pH = 2

   d. $[OH^{1-}] = 1 \times 10^{-7}$ M

   e. pH = 7

6. Calculate pH values for the following solutions. A solution with:

   a. $[H^{1+}] = 1 \times 10^{-3}$ M

   b. $[OH^{1-}] = 1 \times 10^{-9}$ M

   c. $[H^{1+}] = 8.53 \times 10^{-9}$ M

   d. $[OH^{1-}] = 4.21 \times 10^{-8}$ M